IMPROVING YOUR GARDEN

(previously entitled *Making the Most of Your Garden*)

Oliver Dawson writes from long practical experience, having made fifteen different gardens of his own and assisted in the planning and planting of many others. As well as being the author of a number of gardening books, he contributes a weekly column to two evening newspapers and writes regularly for the leading gardening magazines.

He now lives in Surrey and is married with one son.

The picture on the front cover was taken in Brigadier Lucas Phillips' garden by Harry Smith

Small Garden Series

Editor: C. E. Lucas Phillips

IMPROVING YOUR GARDEN

(previously entitled *Making the Most of Your Garden*)

Oliver Dawson

REVISED EDITION

PAN BOOKS LTD : LONDON

First published as *Making the Most of Your Garden*
in 1967 by W. H. & L. Collingridge Ltd.
This revised edition published as *Improving Your
Garden* in 1972 by Pan Books Ltd, 33 Tothill Street,
London, SW1.

ISBN 0 330 02896 0

*Printed in Great Britain by
Cox & Wyman Ltd, London, Reading and Fakenham*

For Patrick

Contents

List of Illustrations

(between pages 70 and 71)

Chapter One

The Heart of the Matter

Any really enthusiastic gardener, on acquiring a new property, should ask himself what kind of soil he is getting with it. But most of us, myself included, never do this. For a variety of reasons, the opportunity seldom arises, but soil conditions play such an important part in the making of a successful garden, that it would be only common sense to take *some* heed, at least, of the type of soil we shall have to tackle; whether we are merely moving house, or making a start, on virgin soil, with the fascinating pursuit of gardening for the very first time.

It is too late to lament the fact that we cannot grow any of the lovely lime-haters – rhododendrons, camellias and many other similar plants – after we have settled comfortably into a house on a chalk subsoil. It could be equally disappointing to the more elderly gardener, or to those to whom strenuous exercise comes hard, to find themselves saddled with a sticky, unworkable clay soil, when they could have coped quite satisfactorily with a light, sandy loam.

This is not to say, however, that soils like these do not have their own particular virtues. A whole host of plants, including stone fruits, ornamental cherries and practically the whole delightful viburnum family, to name only a few, are seen at their best on chalk, while clay soils, once they have been knocked into good shape, are among the best all-rounders for garden purposes on account of their excellent moisture-holding properties during prolonged periods of summer drought. In general, however, we shall have to make the best of what we get, 'learn to live with it' as my doctor tells me when I complain of rheumatism and stiff joints. And if we know a little more of the ways in which our garden soils originated, and of the best methods of bringing them into optimum condition, we shall be much better equipped to tackle a new plot or to maintain an existing one in good heart.

Types of Soil

With the exception of peat, most of our native soils consist basically of mineral particles, varying in size according to the type of soil, which have been formed from various kinds of rock. Originally they were either igneous rocks like granite, basalt and quartz, formed by volcanic action in the earliest days of the earth's history, sedimentary rocks, formed under water by deposits of weathered rock material brought down by floods, rivers and glaciers, or metamorphic rocks, produced under conditions of high pressure and temperature. Sandstone and marble respectively provide examples of these two latter kinds.

Origin of soils. The soil particles can be formed from the parent rock in a variety of ways. Frost and extremes of heat and cold are among the most important agents contributing to this process of disintegration. The expansion of frozen water can exert tremendous pressures, as anyone who has suffered from burst pipes after a severe cold spell can testify. Frost can cause flaking and scaling where rainwater lies on the rock surface, and even fragmentation of porous rocks, where water lodges in natural joints or bedding planes.

Weathering also takes place by chemical and biological means. Carbon dioxide present in the earth's atmosphere forms a weak carbonic acid solution with rain that is capable of dissolving out various minerals from the rock. The activities of earthworms, too, play their part in reducing still further the size of the smaller particles during the process of digestion.

Soil texture. The main soil types found in the British Isles range from almost pure sands to the heaviest of clays. In between these two extremes come sandy loams, light to heavy loams, chalky soils, peat, and enough permutations of these types to puzzle even a football pools enthusiast. Peat is the odd man out on this list. All the others are mineral in origin, but peat is entirely organic, having been formed from vegetation that has undergone a rotting-down process in bogs and swamps.

The texture of the remaining soil types is determined, in general, by the size of the soil particles of which they are composed. Those that constitute a heavy clay are minute. As a result there is very little air space between them and, when wet, they bind together into the solid, sticky goo with which many gardeners are familiar and then dry out into clods of an almost rock-like consistency.

Sandy soils, on the other hand, are made up of quite sizeable grains, which makes them wonderfully easy to work, but causes rapid loss of moisture after rain as well as speedy leaching away of the plant nutrients so vitally important to plant growth and health.

The 'perfect' garden soil, if it really exists, would consist of an admixture of sand and clay in proportions sufficient to make it heavy enough to retain moisture without waterlogging, yet light enough to make it easily workable and to prevent it from drying out into solid lumps.

Fertility. These qualities alone, however, would still not be sufficient. Although it is possible, under controlled conditions, to grow plants in sterile sand, it is still necessary to supply moisture and suitable plant nutrients. Sterile soil, in fact, would be far from suitable for supporting our garden plants in the manner to which they are accustomed, as many of us have found, to our cost, when we have tried to raise a lawn or grow plants successfully in the excavated subsoil that builders have a happy knack of spreading over all the more important parts of the garden when they take out the foundations for a house.

Humus. Soil fertility is dependent, to a great extent, on the presence of sufficient quantities of humus in the soil. Humus is the end product of decaying vegetable and animal matter. Not only does it contain most of the minerals and nutrients necessary to healthy plant life in a readily assimilable form, it also acts as a kind of 'cement', binding the finer soil particles into large crumbs, thus improving the structure of the soil and in particular its moisture-retaining capacity. By the addition of humus, or by encouraging its formation in the soil, we can open up heavy clay soils to make them more easily workable, or improve the moisture-holding qualities of coarse, sandy soils.

How does the transformation of organic waste into this miracle material take place? Nature has staffed our gardens with an unpaid labour force whose personnel number countless millions. It has been estimated that in a handful of soil there can be as many as twenty million living organisms – mostly working towards one end, namely the breaking down of dead vegetable and animal matter, in fact, anything of organic origin, into the material that we call humus.

Earthworms. The first to go to work are the earthworms. A sort of underground pioneer corps, they carry out the heavy initial labour. Their appetites are voracious. Earthworms will swallow almost anything, from dead leaves to earth itself, grinding up the larger particles and vegetable matter into the fine, extremely fertile soil that they excrete in the form of the familiar wormcasts.

They also drag down dead leaves and decaying vegetation from the soil surface and having partially digested these as well, deposit the residue at the lower levels where, having undergone further decomposition, it will mix with other soil constituents to boost the supplies of humus.

Micro-organisms. Although the earthworm population of our gardens may run into many thousands, they are not, as I have said already, by any means the most numerous of the living organisms present in the soil. Yeasts, moulds, fungi, bacteria and protozoa are present in their millions and all play a vitally important role in maintaining soil fertility. Not only are they too numerous to count, many also are too small to be seen with the naked eye and too various to describe in detail.

It is the yeasts and fungi that take over after the preparatory operations of the earthworms. The long white threads that appear in your compost heap or in piles of decaying leaves are the means by which the latter spread, while the yeasts cause fermentation to set in, causing chemical changes and releasing carbon dioxide in the process.

Many of you will be familiar with the nitrogen-fixing bacteria that advertise their presence by the small nodules formed on the roots of peas, beans, lupins and other leguminous plants. The nitrogen which they collect and store in these nodules can greatly enrich the soil for succeeding crops if the plant residues are dug in in the form of green manure. Although the reason for it has not always been understood, this is the basis of agricultural crop rotation, in which a crop of legumes like clover or vetches is used to rejuvenate tired soils whose fertility has been used up by other crops hungry for nitrogen. In the vegetable garden, crop rotation avoids the perpetuation of pests and diseases associated with specific plants, and maintains soil fertility in the process of supplying different crops with their food requirements.

These are just a few of the microscopic organisms present in your soil. There are countless others, all forming part of Nature's 'bucket chain' with whose help she carries on her never-ending cycle of Life ... Death ... Life ...

Improvement of the Soil

There are few soils, if any, whose fertility cannot be improved by careful cultivation and the addition of humus. It is, however, a gradual process that can only be built up to perfection over a large number of years. There is no short cut to soil fertility. This is illustrated very clearly by the rich black soil of old cottage gardens, where regular applications of animal dung stores up fertility, often to a depth of two spits. The gardener who acquires such a soil can count himself fortunate. Let him beware not to fritter this precious legacy away by neglect, careless husbandry or the too liberal use of inorganic fertilizers.

Composting. There should be no need to stress the importance of the compost heap in the present-day garden, or to draw attention to the folly of burning or otherwise destroying any kind of garden or domestic waste that is capable of being composted. It was very different, however, when we first started to garden in the Thirties. We were looked upon as cranks and faddists when our first attempt, by the methods then currently fashionable – they involved, I remember, a mammoth construction using old railway sleepers – saw the light of day in the vegetable garden. This was the Indore process, so strongly championed by the late Sir Albert Howard, in which alternate layers of vegetable waste, manure, earth and lime were used to make a kind of layer cake of compost.

This was certainly a most effective system and produced dark, crumbly, sweet-smelling compost in a very short time – often in as little as six weeks – but the actual process of building and turning the heap could be a laborious and time-consuming operation.

Nowadays, we build our compost heaps in the open, as suitable materials become available, protecting them from excessive rain by a covering of old sacks or, more recently, by the use of polythene sheeting. With the present-day shortage of animal dung, I usually find it necessary to substitute some alternative kind of activator. I rather like the QR method, which was first introduced by Miss Maye E. Bruce, in which a solution containing herbs and honey is watered into the heap as construction progresses. The QR (short for Quick Return) mixture is obtainable in packets in powder form, ready for mixing with water, from garden shops, nurserymen and chemists specializing in horticultural preparations.

There are other equally good proprietary activators, or you can use sulphate of ammonia, sprinkling it generously at about 6-inch intervals while the heap is under construction. For those who are averse to the use of inorganic fertilizers, dried blood or fish meal both make effective substitutes. Where sulphate of ammonia or dried blood is applied a light dressing of lime would be used as a neutralizer provided the resulting compost is not intended for lime-hating plants.

Mulching. Another way to improve the texture and fertility of your soil is by regular mulching. This really amounts to doing your composting *in situ*, and is particularly suited to the shrub border or the fruit garden where the occupants stay put from year to year, and there is room to work among them without damage or disturbance.

Various materials are suitable for using as mulches. These include leafmould, dead leaves, sedge peat, lawn mowings, sawdust, straw and partly rotted compost from the heap. Mulches, in addition to their primary purpose of keeping the soil moist, perform a twofold service; as they are incorporated in the top spit either by a light forking in at the end of the season or by the action of rain and earthworms, they increase the humus content and consequently the fertility of the upper soil layers; they also act as weed smother and prevent any but the most persistent perennial weeds from gaining a foothold.

Mulches should be regularly renewed throughout the growing season – a permanent covering of between 1 and 2 inches should be the target. This treatment is extremely effective in the shrub border and round strawberries, raspberries, currants and gooseberries. For the three last-named soft fruits, a permanent summer straw mulch to a depth of 3 or 4 inches can be used. This not only ensures a constant supply of nitrogen-rich humus for the plants but also makes it easier to get on the surrounding ground in wet spells without causing consolidation of the soil. Since, however, the process of rotting down tends to lock up available nitrogen temporarily, occasional dressings of sulphate of ammonia or fresh manure should be applied at the rate of 2 to 3 ounces to the square yard.

Really successful gardening depends, in no small measure, on our getting to know the soil and situation requirements of the various plants that we grow. These preferences will be examined in greater detail later, but this might be a suitable place to consider the matching of plants to varying conditions of soil, aspect and situation.

Lime-haters. Today, even the proverbial schoolboy must be aware that it is a waste of time and effort to attempt to grow rhododendrons in alkaline soils (except by the use of iron sequestrene). But there are many lesser-known plants with similar likes and dislikes, as well as others that will flourish only in light or heavy, dry or damp, soil conditions.

Some nurserymen, but certainly not *all*, draw attention to these plant idiosyncrasies in their catalogues. If he is unlucky enough to patronize those of the latter kind, the inexperienced gardener could easily find himself saddled with some expensive failures. Among the less well-known lime-haters are the Chilean Firebush, *Embothrium coccineum lanceolatum*, with its brilliant scarlet bottlebrush flowers, the dainty pink-flowered Calico Bush (*Kalmia latifolia*), *Pieris* and *Andromeda* species, and the decoratively berried pernettyas.

The North American Sweet Gum, *Liquidambar styraciflua*, one of the most striking trees for brilliant autumn leaf colour, is among the few deciduous trees with a definite dislike of lime. Among the conifers, too, there are few calcifuges; some, like the junipers, actually benefit from regular dressings of carbonate of lime.

Many of the heaths are lime-haters, but, fortunately, all the varieties of the winter-flowering species, *Erica carnea*, will tolerate the moderately alkaline conditions found in many gardens, so that even if we cannot bring a breath of the moors to our gardens in summer we can at least enjoy the winter heathers' brilliant display during the shortest days of the year.

Shade. For many of us, shade presents another difficult problem. Although many sun-loving plants will make a good showing in conditions of partial shade, it is generally more satisfactory to grow plants that actually prefer shady conditions. There is a wide enough choice to suit everyone's taste, and the matter is dealt with in Chapter Two (pp 10 to 20).

Moist places. Really moist places offer another challenge to the resourceful gardener. Where drainage is difficult or impossible, it is better to make the best of a bad job. Instead of trying to improve matters, make a feature of the site and grow the kind of moisture-loving plants that will revel in the bog-like conditions: primulas, marsh marigolds, dogwoods, willows, alders and the various other plants, trees and shrubs that are seen at their best by the waterside, and are more fully described in Chapter Three (pp 40 to 46).

Dry banks. Rock Roses, brooms, gorse and barberries flourish on hot, dry banks as will most members of the heath family, while for chalky soils the choice is wider than we sometimes realize. It includes perennials such as scabious, pinks and carnations and shrubs like *Buddleia davidii*, deutzias, lilacs, spiraeas and weigelas as well as evergreens like the Mexican Orange-blossom (*Choisya ternata*), hollies, laurels, pittosporum and box and some conifers – cedars, junipers, larch and yew.

It will be obvious by now that we cannot blame soil conditions for a failure to make a satisfactory garden. Choice of suitable subjects, allied to a sustained effort to maintain and improve soil fertility, can make even the most unpromising stretch of ground – to fall back on a well-worn cliché – 'blossom like the rose'.

Chapter Two

Sunshine and Shadow

The garden that is entirely without shade does not exist. Even in a new garden, where the situation is completely open, there will still be the shade from the house walls and boundary fences, while an established plot will enjoy the benefits afforded by shrubs and ornamental trees. On woodland sites (and with the present shortage of building land, there are many more of these being built on), the shade may be dense in parts, while the sun is likely to go off the cleared areas relatively early.

At the opposite extreme, there are parts of many gardens that are sun-drenched from dawn to dusk on fine summer days. To make a success of our planning and planting, therefore, all these conditions must be taken into account. It will be necessary to discover just which plants will thrive in these varying conditions of shadow and sunlight. Too many gardeners write off the shadier parts of their gardens under the impression that nothing will succeed there except a few uninteresting evergreens of the laurel and privet type. Nothing, however, could be further from the truth.

Shade

There are, of course, varying degrees of shade, from the dense, impenetrable shade of conifers and large evergreen shrubs and trees, to the light, dappled shade where the overhead cover consists of deciduous trees of light foliage, such as birch, or the smaller ornamental flowering trees.

A further problem is presented by the dry, shady conditions

at the foot of large trees, where the roots have robbed the surrounding soil of all nourishment and the position is aggravated by the fact that the over-head canopy of leaves prevents almost any rain from reaching the soil surface in the growing season. Here again, however, judicious selection will provide a fair number of plants ready to put up a showing in these inhospitable conditions. In fact, if I were offered the choice between an open, sun-baked plot and a partially-wooded shady one, I would choose the latter every time.

Again, there is the partial shade cast by east and west-facing house walls, hedges and fences, as well as the more permanent shade on the north side of buildings. All of these positions pose their own set of problems, but Nature herself has duplicated such conditions since time immemorial so that, with such a wealth of planting material at our command, it should not be difficult to find the answer to them.

Dense Dry Shade

Let us consider first the most difficult of all the conditions mentioned, the dry, dense shade that is found at the foot of the trunks of large trees, including conifers.

Admittedly, for such situations, the number of plants that are suitable is strictly limited, but the choice is there, for those who care to take advantage of it. But the first thing to do is to improve the condition of the soil by replacing the top spit with some that is more fertile or by the addition of humus-rich compost in bulk. This will counteract, as much as possible, the depredations of the tree roots, and regular treatment of this kind will ensure continuing fertility.

In my last garden, there was a handsome group of Lawson's cypress (*Chamaecyparis lawsoniana*) 30 feet tall, that made a pleasing picture from the house windows. They were beginning to get rather thin at the base and the soil underneath them had been robbed of nourishment.

It would have been a pity to cut them down; their soaring columns did a great deal for the appearance of the garden, framing to perfection one side of a vista that led the eye to a small rose garden, but the dying lower branches and browning foliage were beginning to turn them into what might almost be described as an eyesore.

Mahonias. To cover up the shabby fringes of their skirts, I underplanted the Lawson's cypress with half a dozen specimens of mahonia, using the common form, *Mahonia aquifolium*, sometimes known as the Oregon grape. This North American shrub, with its very early racemes of butter-yellow, primrose-scented flowers, attractive holly-like foliage that turns a rich plum colour in autumn and masses of deep purple berries, is rather looked down on nowadays. When it was first introduced by Douglas in the 1820s, however, it was considered a choice rarity, plants changing hands for as much as 10 guineas apiece. Perhaps it is the ease with which it can be increased from off-shoots that made gardeners revise their opinion of this useful and handsome shrub.

Whatever the reason, there is no finer subject for planting under trees, and the dense 5-foot clumps that my half-dozen quickly formed were soon instrumental in effectively screening the unsightly appearance of my conifers.

Incidentally, the grape-like fruits, tart and astringent, with a bloom like hothouse grapes, are edible and make an excellent preserve if you can get them before the birds do. The glossy foliage remains attractive throughout the year and this shrub would, in fact, make ideal ground cover in any shady position. The variety *aldenhamensis* is taller than the type and there is also another form, *undulata*, which will not tolerate really dense shade but is worth growing for the beauty of its crimped, glossy foliage.

All the mahonias, in fact, do best in partial shade, although *aquifolium* is the only species that will really thrive in the extreme conditions mentioned above. The most outstanding of them, *M. japonica*, has magnificent pinnate leaves of soft green and bears throughout February and March large drooping racemes of golden, lily-of-the-valley-scented flowers. It has a close rival in *M. lomariifolia*, whose habit of growth is more erect, but which is slightly tender in exposed situations. The leaves of the latter are longer and narrower, and the flower trusses are sometimes as much as a foot in length with hundreds of individual florets in each.

Butcher's broom. Another evergreen that will flourish in the densest shade is our native butcher's broom, *Ruscus aculeatus*. Its small, spear-shaped 'leaves' are, in fact, not leaves at all, but flattened stems, known botanically as cladodes. Individual plants are unisexual so that both male and female forms must be planted if we want the bright red berries that decorate the latter.

This shrub gets its popular name from its former use for cleaning down butchers' chopping blocks.

Snowberry and Privet. The snowberry *Symphoricarpos albus laevigatus* is a good shrub for very shady situations, but you are warned that it spreads vigorously by underground suckers. The attractive white mothball berries have the advantage of being left alone by the birds. In winter arrangements, indoors, they contrast well with the polished black berries of the small-leaved privet, *Ligustrum ionandrum*, another shade-tolerant shrub.

All the hypericums make good shrubs for shady situations, including the weed-smothering St John's Wort, *Hypericum calycinum*. These are described more fully on pp 34–5.

Ivy. We generally think of ivies as climbing shrubs, but they can also be used with great success as carpeting plants at the foot of trees, in which situations even the densest of shade will not deter them. It will be necessary, however, if they are used in this way, to ensure that they do not obtain a foothold on the trees themselves.

The common ivy, *Hedera helix*, looks quite effective used in this manner, but I would prefer to employ the variegated *H. colchica dentata* 'Variegata', whose larger, gold-margined leaves give an illusion of sunshine even in the shadiest positions.

One of our most striking garden effects was obtained practically by accident, when we had to find some means of camouflaging an enormous tree stump that protruded, like a badly decayed tooth, from the soil at one end of a shrub border. It was in the full shade of a group of larches and to have had it removed would have caused too great an upheaval among the surrounding shrubs. We decided, therefore, to do a cover-up job and planted, more by way of experiment to see which would be the survivors, the golden ivy just mentioned, some periwinkles (both the large-leaved *Vinca major* and the smaller and narrower-leaved *V. minor*), with, for good measure, one of the cultivated dead-nettles, *Lamium galeobdolon* 'Variegatum'. Results exceeded all our expectations. Within two years, the tree stump was totally submerged in a tangle of contrasting forms and leaf textures – the glossy green and gold of the ivy, the darker green leaves of the periwinkles, studded with their tiny trumpets of soft blue from March to May, and the rough, matt-textured leaves of the dead-nettle with their central markings of tarnished silver.

Sarcococcas. We do not see enough of the sarcococcas, those Asiatic members of the Box family, although they were popular in our grandfathers' day, for covert planting in particular. These evergreen shrubs do well in full shade. *Sarcococca humilis* is the most compact species, growing only 2 to 2½ feet tall with a lateral spread of similar dimensions. Its lanceolate, blue-green foliage is quite handsome. The next tallest is *S. confusa*, at 3 to 4 feet, with smaller leaves of a fresh green. The more vigorous *S. hookeriana digyna*, with willow-like leaves of dark green and attractive purple young shoots, tops them both at 5 feet.

Gaultherias. If, as many of us do, you like to admire the beauty of the tree trunks in winter, you may prefer merely to carpet the ground to the foot of the trees. In this case, no finer evergreen shrub could be found for the purpose than *Gaultheria procumbens*. This North American creeping shrub, known in its native haunts as the Creeping Wintergreen, is the natural source of that soothing but pungent oil of wintergreen, which is used in liniments and medicinal rubs.

Gaultheria procumbens needs a lime-free soil, rich in humus. It will quickly form a carpet of dark green glossy foliage which is studded each autumn with hundreds of bright red berries. An additional attraction is the beauty of the young shoots which, when they first appear in spring, are a striking coral pink in colour.

Dappled Shade

As we emerge from the denser shade into the dappled sunlight underneath deciduous trees or tall shrubs, our choice of plants widens considerably. Given suitable conditions, a relatively well-drained but moist soil with a pH factor of around 6·5 no one, surely, could fail to want to cultivate rhododendrons, those so-called 'Kings of the Garden'. Or could they? I speak from bitter experience, as our present garden is practically a textbook example of the above-mentioned conditions. And yet the previous owner had not planted a single rhododendron because, as she explained when I asked her why, 'she found evergreens depressing'.

To refer to rhododendrons as 'evergreens' – which, of course, they are, in the main – seems to relegate them to the same category as the sooty laurels and grimy privets of the Victorian shrubbery, whereas, of course, they are magnificent shrubs.

One of our first tasks, therefore, when we took over the cottage three years ago, was to dig and plant a long border, in the shade of a mixed group of deciduous trees, with these and other choice lime-haters, including another group of 'evergreens', some of the lovely *Camellia williamsii* hybrids.

Rhododendrons. In the main, we have concentrated on rhododendron species. I have nothing against the lovely named hybrids and have grown them for many years. They are colourful, elegant and easy to cultivate. But our cottage garden is surrounded by woodland which a previous owner planted with hundreds of these magnificent hybrid forms, whose brilliant display no plants of mine could ever hope to emulate in my lifetime. By concentrating mainly on the species, therefore, we had the satisfaction of knowing that we were growing something a little out of the ordinary – and indulging in an innocent form of garden snobbery to which, I fear, many of us are sometimes prone.

Partial shade is essential to most of these species, whereas many of the hybrids are perfectly happy in very light shade, given a cool, moist root run and soil rich in humus. The hybrids mentioned below are those that I have been successful with in my previous gardens, in varying conditions of shade. I cannot claim that they are the finest, or the showiest in cultivation. But they are all, at least, readily obtainable from the stock of any nursery that includes a representative selection in its catalogue.

For the newcomer to rhododendron growing, the so-called hardy hybrids are the least demanding. These are particularly good for new gardens as they will stand up better to exposure and are, as their name implies, completely hardy. Many of them, in fact, have been demonstrating their worth since the second half of last century.

The varieties mentioned, with the exception of *R. praecox* and *R.* 'Nobleanum', come into flower in late May or early June. I particularly admire the whites, which range from the pure white, crimson-blotched blooms of Mrs J. C. Williams to the massive flower trusses, just faintly tinged with pink, of the majestic Loder's White. Cream is well represented by Harvest Moon, which has a central carmine blotch, and Adriaan Koster, whose large flowers have a yellow flare.

Those with a taste for 'shocking' pink are well served by Pink Pearl, whose large, well-formed flower trusses pale to a more delicate shade as the individual florets open. I prefer Mother of Pearl, a sport of the former whose colour begins where that of Pink Pearl leaves off, and finally fades to an almost pure white. Neither of these lovely rhododendrons should be planted in full sun; they will benefit, too, by being sheltered from the wind, as the blossoms are inclined to wilt and turn brown at the edges when subjected to too much sun and wind.

More delicate in colour are the lilac-pink blooms of Betty Wormald, another really old favourite. The individual flowers of this hybrid are large, frilled at the edges, with paler speckled centres. Countess of Derby, a cross between the rosy-crimson Cynthia and Pink Pearl, shows a distinct superiority to both her parents.

Britannia, a compact, slow-growing rhododendron, is still considered by many to be one of the finest reds, but there are others of a purer colour, including Madame de Bruin and Unknown Warrior.

Yellow rhododendrons are as attractive as they are uncommon. The faintly pinkish buds of Goldsworth Yellow open to a soft apricot before turning a clear primrose shade. Prelude, a taller growing variety, has blossoms of pale yellow. Goldsworth Orange, maize-yellow flushed with orange, is very striking but not as hardy as those already mentioned.

Nobody has yet given an English name to my favourite hybrid, although it richly deserves one that is suitably descriptive of its beauty. This is *R.* 'Fastuosum Flore Pleno', a vigorous plant with large loose flower trusses of pale lilac-mauve, whose petaloid stamens make the flowers look as if they are wearing frilled underskirts. For many years now, I have been looking for rooted runners on a large specimen that grows alongside a neighbouring footpath, but none of the stems, although buried deep in fallen leaves, has so far obliged by making roots. This year, therefore, I have finally planted a nursery-bought specimen so that at last we shall be able to enjoy its quiet beauty from the cottage windows.

For more sheltered gardens and milder districts there are two early-flowering rhododendrons that are an absolute 'must'. *R. praecox*, the earlier of these to flower, will produce masses of rosy-purple blooms in February. In all but the mildest districts of Britain, however, you are gambling on the weather if you grow this hybrid. The flowers can be ruined completely by a really severe frost. It is, however, a gamble well worth taking. In a mild spring, this is one of the most colourful and showy of all early-flowering shrubs. For the milder parts of Britain – Cornwall or Western Scotland, for example – it is, of course, ideal.

Rhododendron 'Nobleanum' flowers somewhat later so that its smaller trusses of rosy-scarlet flowers are less susceptible to damage. It also keeps some of its buds in reserve, so that if the first flush of blossom does get damaged, there are others to act as replacements.

Azaleas. Sharing the liking of rhododendrons for acid soil conditions and partial shade are the azaleas, both the deciduous and evergreen species and hybrids. These are, in fact, a race of the Rhododendron genus, so that the common yellow-flowered species formerly known as *Azalea pontica* should be found in catalogues as *Rhododendron luteum*.

It is possible to have a successional display of brilliant colour from the deciduous azaleas from early in May to the middle of June. First to flower are the Mollis azaleas, varieties and hybrids of *R. japonicum* and *R. molle*. These were first raised and introduced by the Dutch firm of Kosters, in the middle of the last century.

Many of the finest of them bear the names of members of the Koster family. The best-known is probably Anthony Koster, a rich yellow azalea whose petals are flushed with orange. Runners-up for popularity include the well-known salmon Hugo Koster and Koster's Brilliant Red, with flowers of an almost fluorescent shade of dazzling orange-red.

The Mollis hybrids seldom exceed 4 feet in height, but the Ghent azaleas grow somewhat taller. Their tubular flowers are sweetly scented and, as an autumn bonus, the foliage of many of them turns to brilliant shades of crimson and scarlet.

The Ghents come into flower at the end of May and from those normally listed I would recommend Gloria Mundi, Willem III and 'Coccinea Speciosa', in various shades of orange. Other excellent named forms are Corneille, Fanny (syn. Pucella), Norma and Nancy Waterer, in shades that range from softest pink to rose-red.

More striking than either of these groups are some of the hybrid strains of more recent origin. One of these, raised and developed by the late Lionel de Rothschild takes its name, Exbury Hybrids, from his magnificent Hampshire garden. The strain contains some of the finest deciduous azaleas in cultivation, with colours ranging from cream through apricot and flame to deepest crimson.

Better known, perhaps, since they have been longer in garden commerce, are the Knap Hill hybrids, which share the same parentage as the Exburys. They, too, offer a wide colour range and fine autumn leaf tints. Worthwhile named varieties include the yellow Harvest Moon; Seville and Tunis, orange and orange-red respectively; and Persil, described as white with a yellow blotch, surely a singularly unfortunate choice of name for any but the whitest-of-white varieties.

Foxgloves. Beds and borders of rhododendrons or azaleas afford ideal conditions for shade-loving perennials and bulbs. Foxgloves are very much at home in this kind of setting and are among the easiest of plants to raise from seed. I have grown only the lovely Excelsior Hybrids since their introduction in the 1950s – the ordinary forms cannot compare with their magnificent colours that range from off-white through delicate pink and crushed-strawberry shades to deep purple and crimson. Unlike the common foxglove, the flowers of the Excelsior strain completely encircle the stems. Once established, plants will seed freely to form large groups. In a woodland setting, where the tiny seedlings can remain undisturbed, they will quickly become naturalized.

Hostas. Hostas, or funkias as they used to be called, are also seen at their best in conditions of partial shade. Their broad, plantain-like leaves, that earned them the name of plantain lilies, make them ideal plants for the margins of a shady border.

Lilies. The acid soil conditions so essential for rhododendrons, azaleas and other lime-hating shade-lovers make their surroundings perfect for growing lilies. *Lilium auratum*, *L. speciosum* and many of the newer lovely de Graaff hybrid strains will all do well provided that drainage is good and adequate. Lilies will fulfil the valuable function of providing welcome colour continuity when the flowering season of the main occupants is over.

Primulas. Although primroses and polyanthus do relatively well in full sun, their preference is really for a moist, shaded position on the fringes of the woodland garden or at the north end of the shrub border. Here, their colours will be more intense and the blooms slower to fade. Also, they will not suffer from those distressing symptoms of wilting, to which members of their family growing in full sunlight are so prone during hot, dry spells in late spring.

Coloured primroses look very much at home among shrubs, and drifts of the newer strains of large-flowered polyanthus will appreciate the shelter afforded from spring gales which often damage their flowers if they are planted in exposed positions. For the woodland or wild garden, however, I prefer the more natural look of our native yellow primrose, *Primula vulgaris*, or one of its improved forms such as Sutton's Yellow. The brilliant colours of the hybrid strains can look out of place in these surroundings, although I would not willingly do without the blue-flowered forms, and grow both Oxford and Cambridge blues, splitting up the plants every other year to provide fresh stocks.

Sunshine

The task of finding plants suitable for sunny positions is obviously much less difficult. In fact, many of the shrubs and perennials that do well in partial shade will give a still better account of themselves when they are grown in full sunlight. The great majority of plants need a sunny, open position if they are to be seen at their best.

Buddleias. Could you, for instance, visualize *Buddleia davidii*, the butterfly bush in any other position than one bathed in sunshine all day, where the brilliant Red Admiral and Peacock butterflies can bask in its warmth as they sip the nectar from the long tasselled flowers? Some garden writers are inclined to be disparaging about this group of shrubs, accusing them of a coarse habit of growth and lack of continuity of interest, but few shrubs give a more generous display – albeit of fairly short duration – for so little attention. What is more, *B. davidii* comes into flower just as the main flush of blossom is over in the shrub border.

Some of the newer varieties are a good deal more striking in colour than the older mauve form that colonized the bomb sites in our cities during World War II, bringing colour and a breath of the country to so many scenes of complete devastation.

Black Knight is a deep, striking violet with long flower trusses, Pink Pearl a lilac-pink with a yellow eye to each tiny floret, and Royal Red, although not as red as its name implies, is a distinctive reddish-purple that may herald the beginning of a new colour range. There are several excellent whites including White Profusion, Peace, White Cloud and White Bouquet.

For those with less space to spare, *B. d. nanhoensis*, which grows only 5 or 6 feet tall as opposed to the 12 feet of the others mentioned, would be an excellent alternative choice. It is bushy in habit, with delicate foliage and flowers of a deep mauve.

Ceanothus. The native habitat of *Ceanothus* is the sunny Pacific coast of the USA. Unfortunately, many of the evergreen species are not 100 per cent hardy in many parts of Britain; however, given shelter from cold winds and really severe frosts – grown, for example, against a south or west wall – they will generally come through even the worst winters unscathed.

In any case, their rich foliage and clear blue flowers, reminiscent of cloudless summer skies, are so attractive that it would be a pity to deny them their place in the sun because of the risk of occasional losses. The more cautious gardener, however, will probably prefer to plant the deciduous species which, in the main, are completely hardy.

The time of flowering varies considerably between different species. Some of the evergreens bloom in May and June, others have a longer flowering season, lasting in some instances from July until October, while others flower early and stage a repeat performance in the autumn.

Ceanothus burkwoodii is probably the best-known of the evergreen forms; it makes a compact rounded shrub and the flowers, of a rich deep blue, appear throughout the summer and autumn. Autumnal Blue, with long-stemmed panicles of porcelain blue flowers, shares these valuable characteristics. *C. thyrsiflorus*, one of the hardiest of the evergreen species, is also the most suitable for growing in bush form in the open, but it is very susceptible to wind-rock and for that reason should have either some form of permanent staking or the shelter of surrounding shrubs to act as a windbreak.

Cascade, one of the newer hybrids, bears, as one might guess from its name, long sprays of powder-blue blossoms on its elegantly arching branches.

Gloire de Versailles, which richly deserves its Royal Horticultural Society's Award of Garden Merit, must be the most commonly seen deciduous ceanothus. Its leaves, larger than those of the evergreen forms, make an attractive setting for the fragrant, soft blue flowers. Topaz grows less vigorously and its flowers are a richer blue; those of Henri Desfosse are darker still. All of these begin to flower in June and carry right through until September or October.

Hibiscus. The name 'hibiscus' always conjures up, for me, tropical sunlight and South Sea Islands, complete with dusky maidens with scarlet flowers tucked behind their ears. Not, in fact, the type of plant that we should expect to find flourishing under our often-clouded summer skies. And yet *Hibiscus syriacus*, the shrub hollyhock, is completely hardy in these islands, and is also extremely valuable in the shrub border, thanks to its late-flowering habit. It normally comes into bloom in August, but flowering can often be delayed until September in inclement seasons.

Its circular frilled flowers – there are both single and double forms – bear a strong resemblance to those of the perennial hollyhock, although they are a good deal smaller. There are many fine named varieties, among which the best of the singles include the large-flowered Blue Bird, Hamabo, a pale flesh pink with a crimson centre, Mauve Queen, William R. Smith, the largest of the single whites, and the striking ruby-red Woodbridge which associates particularly well with a white variety such as William R. Smith, already mentioned.

Lady Stanley, sometimes listed only as *elegantissimus*, is considered to be the best double white, although its flowers are centrally blotched with maroon. Duc de Brabant is a favourite red double, while another, Souvenir de Charles Breton, has flowers of a soft lilac.

Do not worry if your newly-planted specimens fail to produce new young growth when the leaves of other deciduous shrubs are burgeoning all around them. The hibiscus will be among the last of all to put out its light green lanceolate foliage, tarrying sometimes almost until the beginning of June.

Silver-foliaged Plants

Most plants with grey or silver leaves revel in full sunlight. Lavender is, of course, no exception, requiring, as it does, as much warmth and sunshine as possible in order to mature properly the fragrant essential oils that produce its inimitable scent. As far as this is concerned, there is nothing that can touch the Old English or Mitcham lavender (*Lavandula spica*). Unfortunately, this form is much more inclined to legginess than many of the newer varieties; its flowers, too, are of a less intense colour.

Of the deeper purple forms, Backhouse Purple is the most outstandingly fragrant. The dwarf Hidcote is a good deal showier, with flowers of a really deep lavender-blue; these, however, lose in scent what they gain in depth of colour. Gwendolyn Anley, named for that great plantswoman whose garden at St George's Hill, Woking, was long a Mecca for iris-lovers, is an interesting recent introduction, which, coming into bloom later than the other varieties, is distinguished for its almost pink flowers.

Senecio laxifolius, *Olearia haastii* (the Daisy Bush) and *Artemisia abrotanum* (southernwood or lad's love) are all silver-leaved sun-worshippers, as also is the tree purslane (*Atriplex halimus*). Almost all these grey-leaved shrubs do particularly well in seaside districts. Others equally useful for sun-baked situations are *Phlomis fruticosa*, with its outsize, yellow, dead-nettle flowers; the September-flowering *Caryopteris clandonensis*; the cotton lavender (*Santolina chamaecyparissus*), and the grey-leaved Afghan sage (*Perowskia atriplicifolia*), whose stiff, felted stems bear attractive powder-blue flower in August and September.

Annuals

Most annuals have a preference for sunny conditions and although their uses in the garden are many, nothing can compare with an annual border as a striking feature of the summer garden.

Among those with a particular liking for a place in the sun are such old favourites as calendulas, annual chrysanthemums, scarlet flax, Shirley poppies and French and African marigolds. The last-named groups have undergone striking improvements in recent years.

The giant convoluted globes of the modern F_1 hybrids, often as large as the flowers of medium-sized dahlias, are among the most valuable annuals for a long and continuous summer display. They flower from early July until the plants are cut down by frost and have an added advantage in cutting and lasting well in water.

Good named varieties of these newer strains include First Lady, a compact and early-flowering F_1 hybrid with bright yellow blooms $3\frac{1}{2}$ inches across, on 18-inch stems. The Climax strain is taller, $2\frac{1}{2}$–3 feet in height, with large double blooms, 4–5 inches in diameter.

One of the best of the newer French marigolds is Red Brocade, a fine bedding variety with brilliant mahogany-red flowers, centrally marked with golden yellow. Spanish Brocade, a stable companion of the former, has these two colours more or less reversed with yellow predominating.

Phacelia campanularis is a showy hardy annual with bell-like deep blue flowers that grows about a foot tall and is useful either for edging or for the sunny slopes of a rock garden. An even more brilliant blue is displayed by the trumpet flowers of the dwarf convolvulus, Royal Ensign.

An unusual annual, suitable either for bedding or for the back of the border, is the Spider Flower, *Cleome spinosa*. This is half-hardy and grows up to $3\frac{1}{2}$ feet in height. It is so called for the spider-like appearance of its pink flower trusses. The leaves and stems are spiny and the flowers smell rather like spent hops.

Other annual sun-lovers are found among the lovely South Africans – the Star of the Veldt (*Dimorpotheca*) and the Livingstone Daisy (*Mesembryanthemum criniflorum*). Both of these daisy-like flowers have a wide range of brilliant colours and no position in the garden can be too sunny for them.

The first-named is a hardy annual, but the Livingstone Daisy is generally treated as a half-hardy kind and sown under glass for planting out towards the end of May.

Among the more popular annuals that like a sunny situation are nasturtiums and sweet peas, annual sunflowers, sweet-williams and viscaria.

Mixed Sun and Shade

Finally, there are the 'in-betweens', the 'don't-knows' of the plant world, that like a mixture of sunlight and shadow, the latter at their base to ensure a cool, moist root-run and sunshine for their flowers.

Clematis. All the clematis share this rather difficult characteristic, and one way of ensuring that the required conditions are fulfilled is to plant low-growing shrubs, like lavenders or heaths, to shade the plants' nether extremities from direct sunlight.

Another alternative is to plant them on a north-facing corner of a building or on the shady side of a tree trunk. In the first case they can be trained round to the sunny side while, in the latter situation, they will start their life in the shade before scrambling skywards through the branches in search of the sun.

We grow *Clematis montana rubens*, a variety of one of the loveliest and most vigorous species, up an old gnarled apple tree in this way. By this means, the clematis stages a repeat performance after the apple blossom is finished. Hard on its heels come the masses of pink, vanilla-scented flowers of the clematis, which has now climbed twenty feet or more and festoons the topmost branches of the apple with ropes of blossom.

I consider this to be one of the best ways of using clematis and other similar climbers that benefit by 'togetherness' with other kinds of plants. Grown in this way, the climbers need support only until they reach the part of the tree where the branches start to fork. After that, they will scramble quite happily aloft, using the main and side branches as footholds. The value of those picturesque, gnarled old fruit trees that we sometimes inherit, and are so reluctant to sacrifice, is greatly enhanced when they are used as hosts for clematis, vines, wisteria or vigorous rambler roses.

Camellias and tree peonies. These are two other families that need a mixture of sun and shade, although for different reasons. In the case of the former, the flowering period coincides with the season of sharp and severe night frosts, followed often by mornings of bright sunshine that produce a rapid thaw.

It is this that may cause damage. If, however, the sun can be kept off the blossoms so that they thaw out less rapidly, there will be far less chance of damage to the flowers and partly-opened buds. So we plant our camellias in a position facing west, or on a north-westerly wall, where the sun does not get around until fairly late in the morning.

In tree peonies frost damage can occur at an even earlier stage. Their dormant flower buds start to swell at the first hint of warm days in spring, although they do not actually open until May. If we are unable to provide the kind of conditions recommended for camellias, we can effect a compromise by protecting the plants with a light covering of bracken until the danger of these early frosts is past. With young plants, a sheet of newspaper laid over the tops of the plants will suffice. This can be removed when the sun is well up the following morning. As frosty nights are always still and calm at this time of year, there is little risk of this protective covering getting blown away.

Fortunate indeed is the gardener with green fingers, but better-equipped still is one with an intimate knowledge of the likes and dislikes of his plants and their preferences in the matter of soil and situation. It is this kind of knowledge that can turn the average gardener into an enthusiastic and knowledgeable expert.

Chapter Three

Wet and Dry

The fact that a plant is recommended as being best suited to a
sunny position does not necessarily mean that it will thrive in a
really hot and dry situation. Light sandy soils dry out rapidly
in periods of summer drought and even the most copious
applications of the hose or watering-can are not always enough
to satisfy the needs of many plants.

What is more, in many districts the local Water Board vetoes
the use of the hose at these times, when the plants are needing
moisture most, and although even a severe drought is seldom
fatal to the great majority of garden plants, a long dry spell can
play havoc with the summer display.

Hot, Dry Soils

It is advisable, therefore, to provide a quota of plants that will
stand up to drought conditions as an insurance against the
really scorching summers that we always hope for, and occa-
sionally get.

Once again, bountiful Nature has provided us with a wide
choice for this purpose. The plants that come first to mind are
garden forms of the native flora of our heaths and commons –
brooms, heathers and gorse – whose narrow leaves and explora-
tory root systems conserve and search out every available drop
of soil moisture.

Brooms. The name 'broom' actually covers three separate
botanical shrub groups: cytisus, spartium and genista. The
differences between them are too slight to bother any but the
botanists. Between the first two, in fact, the difference lies in

whether or not the seed has on it a slight protuberance. It is useful, however, to know that these distinctions exist when searching for different forms and varieties in nurserymen's catalogues.

Cytisus scoparius is the golden broom of our native moorlands. If it were not so common and so widely distributed it would undoubtedly be greatly in demand as a garden plant. In former times, the broom had a variety of uses, both medicinal and utilitarian, in addition to the one to which it gave its name, the making of brooms or besoms, a method that has been superseded for many years by the use of brooms made of birch twigs. A distillation from its green shoots was formerly used as a powerful laxative, while it was also used for thatching, just as heather is still used in certain districts of Britain today.

It was not until the various multi-coloured forms began to make their appearance that *C. scoparius* obtained a proper entrée to our gardens. Various sports, such as the lovely sulphur yellow Moonlight broom, *C. s.* 'Sulphureus' (syn. 'Pallidus') still a firm favourite, and another with reddish-brown wings to the flowers, *C. s.* 'Andreanus', were among the first to appear on the garden scene, closely followed by many of the lovely hybrids that we still grow today, a number of which are the offspring of *C. scoparius* and the white Portugal broom, *C. albus*.

Among the more outstanding of these are C. E. Pearson, whose flowers are a delightful medley of apricot-yellow and red; Lady Moore, with rich red wings and keel, and buff standards; Lord Lambourne, with wings of crimson-scarlet; and the aptly-named Cornish Cream, which is practically a self-coloured form, with standards of ivory and pale yellow wings.

Several other *Cytisus* species are widely grown as well. *C. praecox*, the earliest of these to flower, produces its masses of butter-yellow flowers towards the middle of April. *C. kewensis*, a dwarf hybrid, growing little more than a foot tall, makes a first-class shrub for the rock garden, particularly if it is allowed to cascade over the edge of a large piece of stone. It is equally effective for clothing dry, sun-baked banks, situations where, in fact, little else will thrive. Like *C. praecox*, it comes into flower earlier than the main body of brooms. The flowers are a pale sulphur yellow.

Garden forms of genista are less numerous, although there are many species indigenous to this country, Europe and North Africa, some of which are as prickly as our native gorse. *Genista aethnensis*, the Mount Etna broom, which originated on the lava-strewn slopes of the Sicilian volcano, has received the Royal Horticultural Society's Award of Garden Merit, an honour which it richly deserves. More like a small tree than a shrub, it grows 10 to 15 feet tall. Its bright green, almost leafless stems are smothered with scented golden-yellow flowers in July.

For banks, the top of a dry wall, or the rock garden, *G. lydia* makes an ideal cover plant. It blooms in May and June, when its downward-curving shoots are a mass of golden blossom. *G. tinctoria* is the dyer's greenweed of former times; it was the source of the green dye which, mixed with woad, produced a colour known as Kendal green. The best garden form is the double yellow, 'Flore-peno'.

This is prostrate in habit, but not as compact as the hedge-hog-like *G. hispanica*, whose bristly hummocks are studded with typical yellow broom flowers in June. The Madeira Broom, *G. virgata*, is unexpectedly hardy for a native of that island; the majority of its shrubs are tender here. *G. virgata* is an elegant shrub, greyish-green with strikingly contrasting flowers of brilliant yellow.

The Spanish Broom, *Spartium junceum*, like many of those already mentioned, takes its name from its country of origin. This is the only example of the genus, and when it was first introduced to this country in the 16th century was known for a long time as the French broom. Its flowers, which are produced in July, are larger than those of the other two groups. Some people might describe its erect and branching habit as leggy. It can, however, be kept more compact by cutting back to the previous year's growth each April.

None of the brooms transplant well, so that they are normally supplied as pot-grown plants. The common broom, *Cytisus scoparius*, is easily grown from seed. Seed sown in pots or seed pans and transplanted to their permanent positions in their second season will often flower the following summer.

Seed of the hybrids does not, of course, come true but will always produce some interesting new colours or combinations of colour. I once stocked a new garden with a few ripe seed pods gathered from a collection of hybrid brooms at Wisley. The flowers of the resulting plants included a variety of lovely colours – maroon, pink, buttercup yellow, milky white, rose and mahogany. Before many years had passed, they were taking up too much room – this was one of our smallest gardens – and many of them had to go to make way for choicer or more exotic shrubs.

But that is one of their great virtues. No shrubs act more effectively as gapfillers while the basic planting is coming to maturity. When they do have to be sacrificed, it is the easiest thing in the world to raise fresh stocks from seeds.

Heathers. Heathers are another valuable group of shrubs for hot dry situations. Additionally, with their ground-hugging, cushion-like habit of growth they will provide almost complete weed cover. This makes them a godsend for the busy gardener with little time to spare for the task of weeding.

The winter-flowering species, *Erica carnea*, is tolerant of moderately alkaline soil conditions, as also are *E. mediterranea*, *E. stricta* (syn. *E. terminalis*) and *E. darleyensis*, but the remaining species, including most of the taller-growing tree heaths, are calcifuges or lime-haters.

Since the winter heaths are by far the most valuable, bringing, as they do, brilliant colour to the garden at a season when it is otherwise conspicuously absent, there is every reason for using them to help furnish arid, sunny spots in the garden.

If the plants are lightly clipped after flowering, they will remain trim and tidy throughout the summer, when the fresh green and bronzy tints of their new foliage will still continue to provide their decorative contribution.

One point should be borne in mind when planting either the summer or winter-flowering species. Although heaths will tolerate, and indeed thrive in, poor thin soils, they appreciate a good start in life, so that it will pay to plant them in pockets of peat or leafmould mixed with a generous lacing of bonemeal. Subsequently, apart from the annual light going-over with shears or secateurs mentioned above, they can be more or less left to their own devices.

A common fault when planting is to use too many single plants of different varieties. Like many other garden plants, heaths make a far greater impact when planted in groups. Those forms of average size will need a minimum of three plants to a group while in the case of a mini-variety such as *Calluna vulgaris* 'Foxii', that grows only two or three inches tall, it may be necessary to put in a dozen plants to obtain the desired massed effect. Only the tree heaths are an exception. These should always be planted singly, so that their erect growth can give a lift to the whole planting.

The heaths, like the brooms, are found under three separate botanical classifications, namely *Calluna*, *Erica* and *Daboecia*. They are a race of shrubs of supreme garden value. It is surprising, therefore, that it is only during the present century that their many virtues have received proper recognition, until today, their trouble-free and labour-saving qualities make them a boon to the gardener with only limited time to give to his hobby. The third genus, *Daboecia*, closely resembles *Erica*.

Many new varieties have appeared in the past ten or fifteen years but few of them, apart from those with coloured leaves, show any outstanding improvement on the older and more widely-grown forms. In our Sussex garden, we concentrate mainly on the winter-flowering Ericas. This is because we have only to walk a few yards from the garden gate to encounter rolling expanses of our native ling in all its summer glory of royal purple. To grow the summer-flowering kinds in the garden, therefore, would be rather a case of 'coals to Newcastle'. Anyone less fortunate, however, would be well advised to find room for some of the summer-flowering species and varieties.

By careful selection, it is possible to have heather in bloom during every month of the year. Among the varieties of the winter-flowering *Erica carnea* that have given me the greatest pleasure are those named after the grandparents of our present

Queen, who were themselves enthusiastic gardeners. *E. carnea* King George and Queen Mary have flowers of bright pink and deep rose-red, respectively.

Other good named forms include the white Springwood, and Springwood Pink, which are both among the best and most rapidly spreading varieties; James Backhouse is a tall, early variety, and Cecilia M. Beale is the finest winter-flowering white of erect habit. I grow as well Vivelli and Ruby Glow for the more lasting beauty of their bronzy foliage; the former has carmine flowers while those of Ruby Glow are a deep red.

Erica arborea alpina, which is sometimes accused of not being completely hardy, came safely through the catastrophic winter of 1962–3 in my Sussex garden. This is one of the finest of the tree heaths and frequently attains a height of 6 feet or more. It bears its long spikes of sweetly-scented white flowers in March, thus neatly rounding off the winter display at the same time as *E. carnea* 'Atrorubra', the latest of the smaller winter heaths to flower, is opening its blossoms of deep crimson-purple.

Those who live on alkaline soils would find it necessary to substitute *E. mediterranea* 'Superba', for the tree heath just mentioned. It is compact and upright in habit, tolerant of lime and grows about 5 feet tall. The flowers, which are borne in great abundance, are a soft pinkish-purple.

The summer display begins with *E. cinerea* and its varieties; these start to flower in June. C. D. Eason, with blooms of a deep lustrous pink, is one of the best known of these. *E. c.* 'Alba major' is an excellent tall white form, while C. G. Best (rose-pink), 'Atrosanguinea' Smith's Variety (blood red), and Cevennes, with close-packed mauve flower spikes, are all well worth growing.

The Cornish Heath, *E. vagans*, which comes into flower in July, will carry the display through to August and September. Two of its loveliest forms are native wildlings, discovered after long and painstaking searches among the vast stretches of the common form that cover the Cornish moors.

St Keverne, with flowers of rose-pink, was run to earth in the locality whose name it bears. Lyonesse, a large-flowered white, was found growing in the neighbourhood of the Lizard. Mrs

D. F. Maxwell, considered by many to be one of the finest heathers in cultivation, has a low, spreading habit and bears long spikes of cerise flowers.

Although I clip most of my heaths as soon as they finish flowering, I would prefer to wait until the following spring to deal with the spent blossoms of *E. vagans*, as they turn an attractive russet colour in winter, to provide a welcome and lasting display against the fresh green of their foliage.

The flowers of the ling, *Calluna vulgaris*, the only species in the genus, are distinctly different from the bell-shaped blossoms of the ericas, being open and star-shaped; technically, *Calluna* differs from *Erica* in having a coloured calyx longer than the corolla. Probably the best-known member of this large company, familiar to gardeners and non-gardeners alike, is the 'lucky' white Scottish heather, *Calluna vulgaris* 'Alba'. Much more showy, however, for garden purposes is the double form, 'Alba Plena'. But by far the most outstanding of all is the double rose-pink H. E. Beale, with flower spikes sometimes exceeding a foot in length.

Crimsons are well represented by C. W. Nix and Goldsworth Crimson. County Wicklow and J. H. Hamilton will provide contrasting shades of pink. There are also many fine varieties of *Calluna* that delight the eye the whole year round by reason of their brilliant foliage. Older ones are *Cuprea* and Searlei Aurea, but these are surpassed by newer ones in glowing tints of gold, copper or bronze, such as Sunset (red in winter), Gold Haze, Bedley Gold, Ruth Sparkes, Joy Vanstone, Golden Feather and John F. Letts. All must be planted in full sun.

Finally, there is the Irish heath, *Daboecia cantabrica*, named for Ireland's St Dabeoc. In this species the choice of varieties is more restricted, and, in general, plants grow about $2\frac{1}{2}$ feet tall, with larger pendent bells than those of the ericas. They have a strong tendency to legginess, which can, however, be counteracted by an annual light clipping each April.

The pure white form looks delightful growing alongside the purple of the type; the latter seems to gain in richness of colour by the contrast. It would look equally well in association with the distinctive variety, *praegerae*, whose pink bells show not even the slightest trace of purple.

Pernettyas. Closely related to and also useful when grown in association with heathers are the varieties of *Pernettya mucronata*, a group of evergreens that are among the showiest of small berrying shrubs. None of them grows more than about 5 feet tall and this, together with their compact habit of growth and closely packed evergreen foliage, makes them useful permanent planting material for frontal positions in the shrub border or for using as focal plants in the heath garden.

The planting holes of these South American shrubs should be dressed generously with peat or leafmould. Most varieties are unisexual so that the type plant *Pernettya mucronata* will have to be planted as well if we are to enjoy the brilliant beauty of the marble-sized berries. But Bell's Seedling, with mahogany-red fruits, and Davis's Hybrids, with berries of various colours, are self-fertile.

Donard Pink bears a profusion of berries of a soft pink, while those of its white counterpart, Donard White, would satisfy the requirements of the most critical of detergent manufacturers. An unusual and attractive form is *lilacina*, whose colour is described in one of my catalogues as Bengal Rose, but which most people would call a light puce.

Hypericums. All the hypericums, including that vigorous spreader and weed smotherer, the Rose of Sharon (*Hypericum calycinum*) will flourish in hot, dry situations. The latter makes one of the finest carpeting shrubs for any garden or soil, spreading rapidly by underground runners. It needs little attention, apart from an annual trim in March to remove weak shoots and the tips of the more vigorous growths. To obtain maximum cover, plants should be a foot apart in each direction. Initial stocks can be easily increased by planting out rooted offshoots. The golden flowers, like outsize buttercups, appear from June to September.

As a specimen shrub for the border, I would prefer to plant one of the named varieties of the *patulum* species. Hidcote has the largest flowers of any of the hardy forms, with golden chalices $2\frac{1}{2}$ inches in diameter. Gold Cup is another outstanding form. It is slightly less tall than Hidcote, reaching an ultimate height of about 5 feet. An added distinction is its autumn leaf colour, when the labiate foliage turns a brilliant shade of pink.

Largest of all are the rich golden-yellow saucers of Rowallane Hybrid which, unfortunately, is not completely hardy. It is, however, ideally suited to the milder parts of the country or will do well if it is given the shelter of a south wall. Left to itself, it will grow 8 feet tall, but makes a much more effective display if it is cut back to ground level each spring.

Grey and silver. Grey and silver-leaved shrubs are notorious sun-worshippers, so that it is hardly surprising that many of them are perfectly at home in arid conditions. Many of these are dealt with on pages 23 and 101–3.

Yuccas. Yuccas might not be everyone's choice for a garden shrub, but their austere, no-nonsense look is very well suited to the restrained planning that is popular with present-day garden designers. They will certainly tolerate conditions that are almost desert-like, and their spiky form would be well suited to a contemporary setting.

One of the most attractive species is *Yucca filamentosa*, so called on account of the threads or filaments that fringe the stiff, sword-shaped leaves. There are two good forms of this, *Y. f. concava*, with an upright habit of growth and *Y. f. variegata*, whose leaves, with their more arching habit and vertical stripes of green, gold and grey, have a slightly less formal appearance.

Yucca filamentosa flowers while it is still young, but others take longer, like *Y. recurvifolia*, with blue-green curving leaves and 4-foot spikes of outsize, ivory, bell-shaped flowers. They are so magnificent, however, that they are well worth the longer wait. The flowers of yuccas should be cut right back when they are over.

The plume poppy. It is useful to have perennials that are drought resistant, particularly in the mixed border, where neighbouring shrubs frequently rob the surrounding soil of much of its moisture. The plume poppy, *Macleaya cordata*, sometimes still listed as *Bocconia*, is one of these. Although it is a member of the poppy family, neither flowers nor foliage bear any resemblance to those of poppies as we usually know them.

The leaves, which are deeply lobed and silvered on their undersides, are more like those of the fig, while the delicate flower trusses, which are responsible for the popular name of this plant, consist of plumes of tiny yellow blossoms. The plume poppy is a first-rate plant for the back of the border as it grows 6 feet or more in height. Its only drawback is its tendency to rapid spread by means of underground suckers; it is a plant that needs careful watching if it is not to over-run its allotted position.

Acanthus. Another perennial that is partial to hot dry positions is *Acanthus*, all forms of which are notable for the great architectural value of their sculptured foliage. It was, in fact, the curves and convolutions of their spiny foliage that were used as a model for the scrolls that decorated the tops of the Corinthian capitals in ancient Greece. *Acanthus mollis* and *A. spinosus* each grow about 3 or 4 feet tall.

Like the plume poppies, acanthus are invasive plants and any scrap of root left in the soil will make a new plant. There is a stretch of cliff just outside Polperro where *A. mollis latifolius*, one of the best garden forms, has escaped from the confines of a neighbouring garden to form an extensive colony on the steep cliffs. The hooded purple flowers of this variety make an impressive sight against the glossy dark green foliage.

Thrift. A plant like thrift, that flourishes in the poorest and shallowest of soils on our native cliffs – a true cliff-hanger, in fact – is a natural for hot, sunbaked positions. Its rounded hummocks of grass-like foliage, closely hugging the ground, make it an ideal edging plant that acts, as well, as an effective weed-smotherer.

There are several improved forms of our native thrift, *Armeria maritima*; these include a dwarf white, 'nana alba', that makes an attractive plant for the rock garden; Vindictive, with flowers of deep reddish-pink more striking than those of the type, and a seldom-encountered variety, 'variegata', whose leaves are golden-yellow.

Anthemis. *Anthemis*, with its masses of daisy flowers in white and varying shades of yellow, makes a first-class plant for a summer border display. Camomile, *A. nobilis*, noteworthy for its medicinal uses – the dried flower heads were widely used in former times for camomile tea – is a member of this family, but it is the taller-growing forms that are of outstanding value as border plants, flowering in July and August. *Anthemis sancti-johannis* is one of these, a free-flowering and popular species with bright orange flowers.

Anthemis tinctoria, the ox-eye camomile, which derives its official name from the fact that the large golden daisy flowers can be used to make a yellow dye, is a species that includes a number of useful named varieties ranging from 2 to 3 feet in height. They will flourish in hot, sunny positions in any kind of soil, provided that it is well drained. Beauty of Grallagh, which seems to be supplanting the older Grallagh Gold as the most popular of these, has delicately cut, ferny foliage of greyish-green and golden-yellow flowers $2\frac{1}{2}$ to 3 inches across. E. C. Buxton is a pale lemon yellow, ideal in flower arrangements using pastel shades; the blooms of Moonlight are paler still. All of these cut and last well – even better if they are initially conditioned by plunging them up to their necks in water for a few hours before arranging them.

Achilleas. Flowering at about the same time of year, and enjoying similar cultural conditions, are two species of *Achillea*, *A. ptarmica* and *A. taygetea*. *A. ptarmica* 'The Pearl', has long occupied a place well up in the plant popularity charts, not only as an extremely effective border plant but also on account of its value for cutting. Its loose corymbs of whiter-than-white, tiny rosettes are just as useful as the flowers of gypsophilia for those who still prefer the more conventional methods of arranging roses or sweet peas. Another good form is Perry's White. *A. taygetea*, with silvery leaves and light yellow flowers, makes an effective contrast to those already mentioned.

Other drought-resisting plants include the brilliant yellow spring-flowering *Alyssum saxatile*, a fine cover plant for dry walls and sun-baked verges, aquilegias, gaillardias and the scarlet *Lychnis chalcedonica*.

As far as the annuals and biennials in more common cultivation are concerned, we shall find that a large majority will thrive better in dry, sunny positions. In many instances, a soil that is too rich, too moist or too shaded will result in a lush growth of foliage at the expense of blossom. This is particularly true of sun-worshippers like calendulas, nasturtiums, wallflowers, French and African marigolds and zinnias, but it is a characteristic shared by many more.

Garden Pools

Mrs Beeton, of cookbook fame is quoted, incorrectly, as having prefaced her recipe for jugged hare with 'First catch your hare'. In the average garden, before we can grow moisture-loving plants, a similar maxim will apply – 'First make your pool'!

Not many of us are fortunate enough to acquire a garden with natural streams, a pond or other water features, including the swampy conditions so necessary for growing bog and waterside plants. Today, however, thanks to revolutionary developments in pool construction, a do-it-yourself water garden lies within the reach of almost everyone's purse and capabilities.

Pool Construction

The old and laborious methods of pool construction in concrete have been to a very large extent superseded in recent years, at any rate as far as smaller gardens are concerned, by the use of materials like fibre glass, PVC, coated terylene or stout polythene sheeting.

Prefabricated pools. Rigid prefabricated pools in fibre glass or plastic are obtainable in a wide variety of shapes and sizes. Installation is simplicity itself. It is only necessary to dig a hole of the required depth and dimensions, drop the ready-made pool into it and there you are, home and dry – or rather *wet*, in this particular instance.

Plastic sheeting. But the method that has fired the imagination of gardeners everywhere and one that is rapidly gaining in popularity on account of its simplicity and economy, is the one in which polythene or PVC sheeting is utilized as a liner for the excavation. These liners are obtainable in almost any reasonable size. Dimensions up to 20 by 20 feet are, in fact, standard, and permutations or combinations of them should be adequate for any small to medium-sized garden. Polythene sheeting, which is used double, is the cheaper of the two materials. It has a life expectancy of approximately two years. More expensive, but with an average life of ten years, is the laminated plastic sheeting, a combination of PVC and terylene, which results in a strong and flexible material with a high degree of elasticity.

Planning and marking. Construction of a pool, using these materials, is a simple matter. First of all, it is necessary to decide on the shape and dimensions. Of the latter, depth is most important; a pool that is too shallow will freeze solid during really cold spells. What is more, it will not be deep enough for certain aquatic plants such as the larger water lilies. The optimum depth for a small pool is between 15 and 30 inches, according to the overall size. Shallower shelves should be provided at the edges approximately 9 inches deep. These will allow for a soil depth of 6 inches, with a 3-inch covering of water, to accommodate marginal plantings.

Once these decisions have been made, the shape of the pool should be marked out on the surface of the ground. Close to the house, formal rectangular, circular or elliptical shapes are the most appropriate, but in other parts of the garden the shape can be more varied and irregular. In all cases, however, it is better to err on the side of simplicity of outline, relying, as Nature herself does, on gentle flowing curves rather than abstruse geometrical designs. Also all pools should be in full sun.

Excavating. The sides of the excavation should be almost, but not quite, vertical and the marginal shelves should have an inner lining of bricks to act as soil retainers. When the excavations are complete, any sharp stones that might puncture the plastic liner must be removed from sides and bottom. The latter should then be covered with a half-inch layer of sand or sifted soil.

Lining. Subsequent procedure varies according to whether PVC/terylene or polythene is being used as a lining. In the former instance, it is merely necessary to lay the plastic over the prepared hole, stretching it fairly taut and allowing a margin of about a foot all round the surface edges.

Bricks or paving slabs, evenly distributed round the edges, will keep the material in position while the pool is being filled. The weight of the water and the elasticity and movement of the plastic will cause the latter to assume the conformation of the prepared hole. Wrinkles may appear at this stage, but most of them will have vanished by the time the pool is full. Any that remain will be unnoticeable when it is fully operative.

Once the filling process is complete, surplus material can be trimmed off round the edges to leave a flat overlap about 6 inches wide all round. This can subsequently be camouflaged with rectangular paving slabs or, in the case of informal pools, with crazy paving or lumps of stone placed strategically round the edges.

With polythene sheeting, the process is very similar, except that, lacking the elasticity of the PVC, it will need to be tailored to fit the excavation before filling commences. This is done by folding it at the corners, moulding it to any curves and making certain that it is in close contact with the pool bottom. A double thickness of heavy duty blue polythene should be used.

Concrete pools. Unlike concrete pools, those made of fibre glass or plastics are ready for stocking with plants and fish as soon as filling has been completed. Those who would like a more permanent garden feature – although concrete pools, too, can leak and crack, particularly with age – will find the booklet *Concrete in Garden Making* (obtainable by writing to the Cement and Concrete Association, 52 Grosvenor Gardens, London, SW1) of the utmost assistance.

Do not forget that the lime in concrete, which is toxic both to water plants and fish, must be neutralized before such pools are stocked. There are several proprietary preparations that will do this effectively.

Water Plants

We shall need three different kinds of plants to furnish the pool and its margins – those which actually grow in the water, bog plants for the surrounding marshy areas, and others for marginal planting which like permanently moist, but not water-logged, soil conditions.

Water lilies. The first thought of anyone who has made a pool is almost certain to be water lilies. Care will be necessary, however, in choosing suitable species and varieties, so that those appropriate to the overall size of the pool are planted. The more vigorous ones would rapidly cover the whole of the surface of a small pool, thus destroying much of its charm which depends, to a great extent, on cloud reflections and the beauty of blue skies and neighbouring trees and shrubs mirrored on its surface.

But there are forms to suit varying depths as well as great and small expanses of water. Some of our native plants are accustomed to growing in water 10 feet deep; we are hardly likely to be able or willing to provide these conditions in the average garden pool.

For the very shallow pool, or for growing in tubs or barrels, *Nymphaea tetragona*, which can manage in as little as a foot of water, is the best choice. This attractive plant has white flowers. *N. pygmaea helvola*, which is the smallest water lily, bears an abundance of sulphur yellow flowers, while those of the named variety Hyperion, are red.

For the more normal depths of 2 to 3 feet, I know of no more attractive water lily than James Brydon, of which there is a very fine example in one of the formal pools that flank the south-west side of the laboratories at Wisley. Its crimson, globular flowers are fully double and outstandingly lovely. Conqueror is a free-flowering red hybrid with strikingly contrasting golden stamens; Gladstoniana, a particularly fine and fragrant white, needs plenty of water surface to spread itself.

Other water plants. Other subjects suitable for planting actually in the water include the water hawthorn, *Aponogeton distachyus*, with narrow elliptical floating leaves and white scented flower trusses; the flowering rush, *Butomus umbellatus*; our native water violet, *Hottonia palustris*, whose lavender flowers break surface while the leaves stay submerged; the Japanese arrowhead, *Sagittaria sagittifolia* 'Flore Pleno', and the Lizard's tail, *Saururus cernuus*, both of which have interesting foliage and white flowers.

Iris laevigata, unlike *I. kaempferi*, does not mind getting its feet really wet, and will tolerate a few inches of water over its roots. The flowers of the type have falls of a brilliant violet-blue. There are, in addition, many exciting named varieties such as the deep purple Regal, the ethereally white Snowdrift, and 'Elegantissima', whose white-striped sword foliage and pale blue shapely flowers could well have inspired some of the *art nouveau* designs that are enjoying such renewed popularity nowadays.

Rushes of some kind would seem to be an appropriate furnishing for the garden pool, and of them all surely the bulrush is the most attractive. Unfortunately, the commoner forms are both too tall and too invasive for the small to medium-sized pool. There are, however, two miniature species – *Typha laxmannii* (syn. *T. stenophylla*), whose brown spikes are only 3 feet tall, and the even smaller *T. minima* which grows to a height of only 18 inches. (These are what most people call bulrushes; in gardening books the name usually refers to *Scirpus lacustris*.)

The Bog Garden

The bog garden can either be incorporated in the marginal planting scheme of the pool itself, or it can be made an entirely separate garden feature. The requirements of most bog plants can be simply stated: in winter and summer alike, they need soil that is permanently wet, but not actually waterlogged, although many bog plants will tolerate water at their roots for considerable periods.

By constructing a bog garden on the fringes of an ornamental pool, the attraction of the latter is greatly enhanced, but anyone without a pool who has a patch that is naturally on the marshy side, or one that can be maintained in this condition artificially either by the damming of a small stream or by trickle feeding from some other source of water supply, can grow the many moisture-lovers that revel in these soggy conditions. In some cases the overflow from the pond can be channelled to create the boggy conditions in the adjacent soil. In such positions, astilbes look particularly fitting. This perennial is one that is seldom seen to its best advantage unless it is grown where the roots have permanent access to liberal supplies of water.

Astilbes. Often mistaken for Spiraeas. There are many outstanding named varieties. I grow what I consider to be the three best reds; Fanal (blood-red), Red Sentinel, whose flowers are the colour of a turkey's wattles, and the deep crimson Etna. Perhaps the brightest colour of all, however, is provided by William Reeves, whose feathery flower trusses are almost scarlet.

Peach Blossom and Venus have plumes of peach and flesh pink respectively, while Bridal Veil is an attractive white that amply justifies its name. Its loose, lacy flower clusters are borne on tall, sturdy spikes.

From the point of view of garden decoration the beauty of the finely-cut, fern-like foliage of the astilbes is almost as important as that of their flowers. In many varieties, this starts off in the spring a bright coppery-crimson, turning green as the season progresses and in some cases colouring brilliantly again to a rich rust or cinnamon in autumn. All the varieties mentioned above flower in June and July and grow between 2 and 3 feet tall.

Marsh marigolds. Flowering earlier, in late April and early May, is one of the loveliest of our native bog plants, the kingcup or marsh marigold. The wild form has single flowers, but I prefer to plant the double, *Caltha palustris* 'Plena' for the more striking show that it makes in the garden. The single kind, however, is equally beautiful as a cut flower and, as might be imagined, lasts extremely well in water. There is also a white variety, *alba*, and I have seen a form with larger double flowers mentioned, *C. p.* 'Monstrosa Plena', although it is not listed by any of my favourite nurserymen.

The marsh marigolds are among my favourite waterside plants. Early in spring, their leathery, high-gloss foliage springs up, bursting with vigour, all along the banks of our little stream, and the butter yellow flowers are out in time to compete with the last of the narcissus and jonquils. Marsh marigolds look very effective interplanted with the water forget-me-not, whose blue flowers complement the yellow of the kingcups.

The bog arum. As far as catalogue listings are concerned, it would be easy to confuse the marsh marigold, *Caltha palustris*, with another bog plant, the bog arum, *Calla palustris*. But in appearance and character no two plants could be more different. The bog arum is a smallish plant with heart-shaped leaves that bears small greenish-white spathes, similar to those of an arum lily proper, during the summer months.

Lysichitums. Similar in appearance, but built on much more majestic lines, are the lysichitums, of which there are two species, *Lysichitum americanum* and *L. camtschatcense*. The former, a native of North America, is known in the United States by the impolite title of Skunk Cabbage on account of the foxy smell of its flowers – exotic-looking yellow spathes with spadices of lime green more than a foot long. The flowers are followed by an abundance of lush green paddle-shaped foliage.

The Asiatic species is almost identical in everything but height and flower colour; the flowers are white and bear a greater resemblance to those of the arum lilies themselves.

Gunnera. Where there is plenty of space, no waterside planting would be complete without a plant of the so-called giant rhubarb, *Gunnera manicata*. Space, however, is the operative word where this fantastic plant is concerned, since the stout stems, which are armoured with wicked spines, can easily grow 6 feet tall in support of the toothed spiny leaves, 6 feet and more across. The flowers, which are turkey red and look like king-sized flue-brushes, make the appearance of this plant even more striking when they appear in July and August, and persist until the foliage is cut down by the autumn frosts. In the smaller garden, it can be restricted by lifting and re-planting one or two crowns only, every two or three years.

Gunnera manicata has the reputation for not being 100 per cent hardy here. As a precautionary measure, it is advisable to give it a protective covering in winter, either of its own dead foliage or of straw, bracken or similar materials.

Rhubarbs. A similar effect of lush growth can be achieved, on a less spectacular scale, by planting one of the decorative species of rhubarb proper. These close relations of our culinary rhubarb include *Rheum rhaponticum* and *R. palmatum*, as well as a striking form of the latter with brilliant red leaves and stems, *astrosanguineum*. These, also, may be too large for the really small pool, but there is a dwarf species, *R. alexandrae*, which would be suitable even for the smallest of water gardens.

Other outstanding foliage plants for bog or waterside are *Rodgersia pinnata*, whose leaves resemble those of a horse-chestnut although the plant is a perennial, and the hostas, or plantain lilies, which are discussed in more detail in Chapter Eight (p 91).

Dogwood. Everyone must be aware of the value of the scarlet stems of the dogwood, *Cornus alba*, as a livener-up of the winter garden scene; to enjoy the brilliance of their colour to the full, however, the improved Westonbirt Variety should be planted. In the form known as *C. alba sibirica* 'Variegata' the scarlet stems are clothed with delightful silver-variegated foliage in summer, making it a useful dual-purpose shrub for those with little space to spare. As a winter contrast to the scarlet-twigged forms, the lime-yellow winter bark of *C. stolonifera flaviramea*, the yellow-stemmed dogwood, can be extremely effective, but it may be somewhat rampant for a small garden.

Primulas. Nobody who has the necessary boggy conditions should fail to grow the delightful bog primulas. They are simplicity itself to raise from seed in a manner similar to polyanthus and primroses, and soon form colonies if their own self-sown seedlings are left undisturbed. Two of the easiest species to raise in this way are the candelabra primulas – *Primula bulleyana* and *P. beesiana*. The former has golden-yellow candelabra flower spikes; those of *beesiana* are a bright magenta.

Equally attractive are some of the hybrid strains of *P. japonica*, which are obtainable in a wide range of reds as well as terra cotta and white. These, too, seed themselves freely and will soon naturalize themselves in any permanently moist patch of ground. Slightly less vigorous and more delicately constructed, *P. pulverulenta* has its flower stems dusted with a silvery farina, like the 'flour' that characterizes many auriculas, such as the old favourite, Dusty Miller. The Bartley strain of primulas is a particularly fine one. It contains a range of brilliant colours in which various shades of pink predominate.

Pool Accessories

The design of the water garden can be elaborated even further by the construction of artificial streams and waterfalls or by the inclusion of a fountain in the pool itself. Few gardens contain the necessary slopes and gradients that would permit features such as these to be self-operating. Also, restrictions on the use of water from the mains could soon dry up these artificial rills and babbling brooklets during periods of summer drought. In consequence, it will generally be necessary to use a pump to circulate the water on a return system.

Pumps. An electric centrifugal pump kit, capable of operating a fountain, waterfall or small cascade can be obtained for less than £10. More elaborate installations, that will serve simultaneously several water features, are naturally more costly, and larger pumps can cost anything up to £50 to install.

Livestock. Pools should be stocked with fish, fresh-water snails and other livestock which will assist in aerating the water, and, by acting as scavengers, help to keep it clear as well. Like the pump units, these are obtainable as 'kits' suitable for differing pool sizes, from the same firms that specialize in garden pools and accessories.

Chapter Four

Views and Vistas

Design and layout play a vitally important role in the garden. It does not matter whether your plot is large or small; even the tiniest garden can be transformed – and for the better – by careful planning.

Pleasing effects seldom just happen. In the great majority of instances they are the result of careful contriving. For instance, every downstairs window should frame a worthwhile garden picture; just as every garden should include some element of surprise.

There are many ways by which these objectives can be achieved. Interior hedges, curving borders, specimen trees and conifers placed at strategic points can all play their part. Even outward jutting wings of trellis or wattle, used as a temporary screen until hedging plants take over, can intensify the feeling of anticipation as we make the 'tour' of the garden.

Round every corner we may come across something new and exciting – the first opening bud on a new rose, the nose of lily bulb thrusting through bare brown earth, or the shimmer of a pool of the sapphire blue Siberian bluebells, *Scilla sibirica*.

To achieve worthwhile effects may take several years, so that it will be necessary to plan ahead with imagination and forethought. These two qualities, however, are not enough; to be able to plan effectively for the future, we shall have to acquaint ourselves with the ultimate height and spread of the plants we intend to utilize.

Use of hedges. As far as hedging plants are concerned this is a comparatively simple matter. Although the majority can be clipped to the desired height and thickness, it is as well to remember that some, like the shrubby honeysuckle, *Lonicera nitida*, should not be permitted to exceed 4 to 5 feet in height or they will become bare and ragged at the base; while the knowledge that others, like yew, holly and box, may take as many as ten years to attain the desired height, could lead to second thoughts as to their suitability for the purpose in hand.

Surroundings. The way in which our views and vistas are planned will depend very much on our immediate surroundings. Do we want to include the latter in the overall garden picture, or are they so uninspiring that it would be better to screen them entirely from sight ? If we are lucky enough to have rolling pastures, hills or woodland as our garden background the obvious thing to do is to arrange a merger and consolidate our good fortune by bringing them into the general garden scheme.

If, on the other hand, our outlook consists of other peoples' gardens and houses, walls, sheds or other unsightly objects, effective screening by means of trees and hedges will obviously be necessary.

Borders. With garden features such as annual or perennial borders, the most striking effect is obtained when they are viewed along their length. In this way, the fullest impact of the various colour groupings and plant textures is achieved.

Smaller formal beds, however, are usually designed to be looked at from above so that the plants used in bedding schemes will have to be carefully graded in height and fairly low-growing in habit. I noticed a good example of this recently at a roundabout on the outskirts of Portsmouth. A circular bed, on a sloping bank practically at eye-level, had been mass planted with wallflowers. If taller-growing varieties had been used, the effect of a flat disc of colour would have been ruined. Instead, by using Golden Bedder, a very dwarf variety that grows only 9 inches tall, the planting gave the impression of a golden medallion resting on a cloth of green velvet.

Garden seats. Garden seats make useful vantage points for the enjoyment of views and vistas in comfort. The type of seat used for the purpose should be so constructed as to be able to be left out in all weathers. Stone seats, although they may be all very well for the large garden, can be too ostentatious for more restricted quarters. Teak is probably the best and longest lasting material, while for an informal setting a length of split log supported on two uprights can be extremely effective as well as being economical. This type of seat, which is widely used in the Royal Horticultural Society's garden at Wisley, is particularly suitable in the wild or woodland garden.

Another kind of permanent garden seat is the park-bench type with an iron frame and wood-slatted seat and back. These can sometimes be picked up for a song at sales and it is surprising how attractive they can be made to look after a few running repairs and a coat or two of black or white paint. Incidentally, avoid using green paint in the garden. It is often recommended as toning with the natural background but the green has yet to be invented that does not stick out like a sore thumb among the varied greens of plant foliage. Black or white blend much more naturally, and I would always use them in preference to green.

Cast-iron garden furniture of Victorian vintage that, ten years ago, people were only too glad to get rid of, has suddenly become madly fashionable with the smart, glossy magazine set and the price has sky-rocketed accordingly. Its formalized patterns of flowers, foliage and branches can be very attractive in a period setting, but for the contemporary house and garden I would choose modern examples of a more restrained design, in wrought iron.

Seats of similar design, copied from classic patterns, are now obtainable in aluminium which makes them not only featherlight to lift, but also completely rust-proof.

Hedges

Without interior hedges, walls, fences or some other type of screen, the element of surprise can never really be present. If we can see the whole of our garden at a glance, the picture tends to be uninteresting. There is, fortunately, a very wide choice of planting material for hedges of varying heights, some of which is even suitable for the pocket-handkerchief plot. The plants used do not need to form as dense or impenetrable a barrier as those utilized for boundary hedges. Other factors influencing the choice of plants are the soil, situation and cost.

Preparation of soil. It is a common mistake to imagine that hedges can be planted in any sort of hastily prepared site without regard to the condition of the soil. To make a strong-growing, dense and attractive hedge, each individual plant should be treated almost as if it were a specimen shrub. In other words, the bed should be double dug or bastard trenched and plenty of humus-forming material should be incorporated in both the upper and lower spits. Shortly before the actual planting operation, a dressing of bonemeal, at the rate of 2 to 4 ounces to the square yard, should be lightly forked into the surface, or alternatively a generous handful can be sprinkled in each planting hole when the plants are set out.

Soil. Choosing a hedge to suit the soil is very important. We can modify our soil conditions to a certain extent to suit individual shrubs, but it would be well-nigh impossible to do this where the site for the average hedge is concerned. The common rhododendron (*R. ponticum*) makes an excellent evergreen hedge, for example, in moist acid soils, but would be a complete write-off in alkaline soils. Beech, on the other hand, is far more successful on chalk, particularly for hedging; the leaves colour better and remain more attractive in winter.

Those who garden in a restricted space may prefer to plant hedges that make a colour contribution to the garden as well as fulfilling their function as screen or shelter. We are well served by many deciduous and evergreen flowering shrubs that make first-class hedging subjects.

Barberries. Among the latter the barberries provide some outstandingly useful material whose close, compact habit of growth makes them ideal as windbreaks. The vicious spines with which so many are armed render them virtually impenetrable by man or beast.

Two of the best evergreen species for hedging purposes are *Berberis stenophylla* and *B. darwinii*, the latter will make a hedge about 6 feet tall; *stenophylla* can top this by several feet. *B. stenophylla* presents a wonderful spectacle in April and May, when every arching spray is massed with brilliant orange-gold blossom. These flowering shoots should be cut back – preferably with secateurs – after the blossom has faded.

Berberis darwinii is somewhat less vigorous but no less attractive in flower. It needs less drastic pruning, so that it is possible to enjoy the beauty of the purple fruits that follow the flowers.

Laurustinus. For a really early display of blossom, there are few, if any, evergreen hedging shrubs to rival the popular laurustinus (*Viburnum tinus.*) This old favourite thrives in practically any soil, situation or district and the pink-budded flower trusses start to show colour in early winter and open in batches during every mild spell until the main generous flush of blossom comes in February or March. After that it is the turn of the attractive young foliage, clear green and borne on red stalks.

Pruning, which should be fairly light, is carried out in spring, after flowering has finished. The plants should be put in 18 to 24 inches apart and planting, as in the case of practically all evergreens, should be carried out either in September/October or March/April.

Escallonia. Escallonias can make one of the most attractive flowering hedges but grow very broad. Although commonly recommended for seaside districts, escallonias will do well in sheltered districts in many other parts of Britain and there are few hedging shrubs with foliage to rival the polished beauty of their dark green leaves.

For sheltered places I would choose *Escallonia* Donard Seedling, with rich pink blossom. This is one of the loveliest, but the hardiest is *E. langleyensis*, which has cherry pink flowers. This is hardy even in the north of England. *E. macrantha* and its varieties are best restricted to mild or maritime districts. One of the loveliest hedging forms is Slieve Donard, whose long arching sprays are massed with large pink flowers. The planting distance is between $2\frac{1}{2}$ and 3 feet and most varieties, if pruned lightly after flowering, will oblige with a second flush of bloom in early autumn.

Forsythia and flowering currant. Deciduous flowering shrubs offer a wider choice of easy-to-grow material suitable for hedging. Two popular shrubs, always found in nurserymen's 'collections' are among the first that come to mind – forsythia and ribes, or flowering currant.

Both *Forsythia intermedia* 'Spectabilis' and *F. viridissima* make excellent hedging plants, while *F. intermedia* 'Vitellina' enhances the beauty of its yellow flowers with twigs of a similar colour. Forsythias should be cut back after flowering as they bloom on the previous season's wood.

I would not recommend forsythias where bud-stripping birds are troublesome. Regularly each spring I find my bushes laid bare of blossom buds by the ravages of bullfinches, and since the attacks frequently occur before Christmas, I seldom manage to apply preventive measures in time. Flowering currants, on the other hand, never fail to put on a brilliant display with their gem-like clusters of ruby flowers set among the delicate green of the just-opening leaves.

Like the forsythias, *Ribes sanguineum* is perfectly at home in almost any soils and is equally happy in town or country. The two most striking forms are *R. s.* 'Atrosanguineum' with flowers of a richer crimson than the type, and the lovely named form King Edward VII, noteworthy for the size of its flower trusses.

Roses. Many roses make first-rate hedging material, but sweetbriers and the Penzance briers, often recommended for this purpose, are very susceptible to mildew and my own preference would now be for the rugosas, hybrid musks or some of the more vigorous floribundas such as Iceberg, Chinatown or Dorothy Wheatcroft. That great all-rounder, Queen Elizabeth, also makes a good hedge provided it is pruned back annually to within 18 inches of soil level.

I have also used the thornless rose Zephirine Drouhin to good effect for hedging. It is extremely vigorous and could be planted at intervals of 6 feet if the initial training is done on wires or a fence. The absence of thorns reduces the hazards of pruning considerably.

Brooms. As mentioned already, brooms are ideal for hot hungry soils. On light sandy soils they will make effective, although relatively short-lived hedges. Brooms transplant badly so that it is important to use pot-grown plants. Planting should be at 3 to 4 feet intervals.

Pruning must be carried out with the utmost care. Prune too lightly and the plants get leggy; too hard and the cut branches die back. I have always found the advice of an old gardener of ours to be remarkably sound. Never cut back into old wood and never cut where the shoots are thicker than a lead pencil. If you follow this maxim you can have a broom hedge that will be a thing of beauty and a joy, if not for ever, at least for ten years or more.

Among the best for hedging is *Cytisus battandieri*, a Moroccan species whose habit of growth is less straggling than most. The soft yellow flower spikes have a scent of pineapple.

Deutzia and Weigela. Many shrubs that are more often thought of as specimen plants can be pressed into service to make beautiful and colourful hedges. Deutzia and weigela both do well in most types of soil, while the former will thrive in a partially-shaded position as well as in full sunlight. All the well-known species and varieties make good hedging material, including *Deutzia longifolia veitchii* (pink), the double white *D. scabra* 'Plena' and its pink counterpart *rosea*. Of the weigelas the two most popular varieties (formerly called diervillas), Abel Carrière (deep pink) and Eva Rathke (crimson), together with the white 'Candida', are all good. Any of these shrubs will make a hedge between 6 and 8 feet tall. Plants should be spaced 3 to 4 feet apart.

Firethorns. Berries, as well as blossom, can do much to enhance the decorative appearance of a garden hedge. I have had great success with two of the firethorns, *Pyracantha coccinea* 'Lalandii' and *P. angustifolia*, with berries of coral-red and orange-yellow respectively. *P. atalantioides*, however, proved a complete write-off as a hedge, possibly due to unfavourable soil conditions, as it is frequently recommended for hedging.

Planting distances are from 3 to 4 feet and once the desired height is attained – which can be anything up to 8 or 10 feet – subsequent pruning will consist of cutting back in late winter or early spring the arching shoots that have borne the berries. I generally wait until the thrushes and blackbirds have eaten their fill, which, in my district, is usually towards the end of January.

Cotoneasters. *Cotoneaster simonsii* is another berrying shrub that makes a first-rate hedge. Unlike the firethorns it is only semi-evergreen but compensates for this by the fiery brilliance of its autumn leaf colour. *C. franchetii*, which is evergreen, with deep green leaves, silvered on the reverse, is equally valuable, and either species, planted 2 to 3 feet apart, will make a striking 8-foot berried hedge.

Conifers. Where a new garden is concerned, the greatest need will probably be for a quick-growing boundary hedge to provide shelter and privacy as soon as maybe. The cheapest plants for this purpose are quickthorn and myrobalan plum, both of which make effective summer screens, but tend to be less efficient after the leaves have fallen. For all-the-year-round privacy conifer hedges of fast-growing habit such as *Chamaecyparis lawsoniana* or *Thuja plicata* are preferable.

Lonicera. *Lonicera nitida* and the somewhat hardier *L. yunnanensis* are excellent and inexpensive evergreen subjects for small gardens. They clip well, and must, indeed, be trimmed regularly and often if they are not to become leggy at the base. They are an improvement on the common privet but are not in the same class as yew, box or holly, all of which, restricted to 6 feet or even less, make superb hedges for any garden.

Those with a craving for complete and utter privacy or who have unsightly neighbouring buildings or surroundings to hide may favour denser and taller hedges. In these circumstances, coarser growing, more vigorous subjects will be called for.

The common hazel, *Corylus avellana*, or its purple-leaved variety, fulfils most of these requirements. The former is quite inexpensive. Hollies, laurels, lilacs, beech and hornbeam will all make a dense hedge 10 feet or more in height, provided they are kept well trimmed and not allowed to develop bare patches at the base.

A path of grass, brick or paving, bordered by low hedges on either side, is useful for leading the eye to some particular point of interest, such as a garden statue, a fountain or other ornament, or even a gap in the boundary hedge that frames a more distant view. For sunny situations, grey-leaved shrubs, such as lavender (the old-fashioned Mitcham lavender makes one of the best hedging varieties) rosemary or cotton lavender (santolina), are all suitable and effective. For shady walks in woodland one or other of those two outstanding hypericums, Gold Cup or Hidcote, planted at 18-inch intervals, would make a low-growing hedge of great charm.

Although the open-plan design, applied to front gardens, can greatly improve the appearance of a housing project and give an effect of space, the average Englishman likes his privacy too much to extend this idea to other parts of the garden. He would rather be completely boxed in by hedges and fences than make his garden an integral part of a communal scheme, a procedure that is greatly favoured both on the Continent and in the USA.

I for one could not blame him, being myself a staunch supporter of the 'Englishman's home is his castle' theory. But with the smaller present-day gardens, hedges and screens are of greater importance than ever before, if we want to avoid living in our neighbour's pockets, and unfortunately, the smaller the garden, the taller and more impenetrable they will have to be if they are to fulfil their purpose successfully.

It is up to every one of us gardeners, however, to try to avoid erecting anything that is unsightly, or that can give undue offence. Good neighbourliness, after all, is as important as the desire for privacy, so we must try not to offend by putting up the kind of dividing hedge or screen that we should object to ourselves if we happened to be on the receiving end.

Fences. Fortunately, there are plenty of attractive screening materials obtainable. My own first choice would be wattle, although the reverse side of hazel wattle presents a somewhat raw and unfinished appearance until it weathers. If you value your 'good neighbour' relations, it might be better to use the more expensive osier panels, which are not only neater, but also afford greater privacy. Various forms of interlap fencing make a neat and tidy screen which, however, can be rather austere-looking before its severity is relieved by climbing plants. Open trellis with climbers offers another solution, but the trellis needs to be very firmly fixed to stand up to strong winds and the dead weight of the growing material.

Chapter Five

Space and Time

This chapter, as its title might at first imply, does not deal with science fiction. It is not only the cosmonaut who is concerned with these two measurements. They are, in fact, extremely important to the gardener who is determined to realize the fullest possibilities of the area and leisure at his disposal.

In the small garden, every square foot of ground must be made to count for something. It is essential, too, to provide for a worthwhile display of either flower, foliage or berry for as long a period of the year as possible.

Making the most of the space however, does not mean that every inch of the garden has to be jam-packed so full of plants that there is no room left for anything else. In any garden, no matter how small, we still need room to relax, even if it is only a few feet of lawn or paving to put our garden chairs on.

Paving

A tiny garden, and practically all town gardens, will benefit from being paved, as also will the majority of suburban front gardens. Too small an area of grass cannot stand up to the wear and tear of frequent use and, as far as the front garden is concerned, it is nice to be able to forget the regular summer chores of grass cutting.

Natural stone or bricks are the best materials, of course, to use for paving, but the price of these two keeps rocketing and most of us will have to be content with prefabricated slabs of artificial stone. They can be almost as attractive as the real thing, particularly after they have had a chance to weather.

And they are so reasonable in price nowadays, that I can really
see no valid reason for anyone making their own from concrete
unless they have unlimited time and energy at their disposal.
These prefabricated slabs are obtainable in a sufficient variety
of colours, sizes and surface textures to satisfy even the most
critical gardener, and are easier to lay than those of natural
stone, since they are all of uniform thickness. If the site to be
paved is carefully prepared and made perfectly level, the actual
process of laying them is child's play.

Laying paving. A 2-inch layer of sand or sifted ash will
simplify the task of bedding them down; filling the joints with
a 3 to 1 mixture of sand and cement will provide a neat finish.
Alternatively, if the idea is to grow creeping plants in the
crevices, the spaces between the slabs can be filled with finely
sifted soil – sterilized as well, if possible.

This can be brushed in with a stiff broom. Remember,
however, that weeds, as well as the prostrate plants of your
choice, will take hold in the crevices, so think carefully before
you decide on this course of action.

Use of Height

Where horizontal space is restricted, a new dimension can be
added to the garden by going upwards. Climbing plants on
pillars, pergolas, walls and fences take up a minimum of ground
space in relation to the display that they provide.

Some people are reluctant to grow plants on their house walls
on account of possible damage to brickwork and foundations.
The majority of climbers, however, have an insufficiently extensive root system to cause any serious trouble to the latter,
while as far as the walls are concerned, it is a simple matter to
erect trellises in such a way that they can be taken down and
replaced if decoration of the wall surface is necessary.

Climbers

Pillars and pergolas, too, make first-rate supports not only for
roses but also for other climbers such as wisteria, honeysuckle,

jasmine and clematis. Two of the most striking that I know that lend themselves to this method of cultivation are the giant vine, *Vitis coignetiae*, and the exotic Asiatic climber, *Actinidia chinensis*. Both of these shrubs have magnificent foliage, with individual leaves 8 inches or more across.

The Passion flower. South and west walls afford excellent opportunities for growing the more exotic climbers. Among the loveliest of these is the Passion flower, *Passiflora caerulea*, whose flowers were endowed with a religious significance on its introduction to this country at the end of the seventeenth century. The ten greenish-white petals and sepals of the corolla are said to represent the Apostles, with Judas and Peter omitted, the striking purple corona, the crown of thorns, while the three stigmas are the nails and the five golden stamens are the five wounds. The leaves and tendrils are the whips and scourges of our Lord's persecutors. All in all, the Passion flower is a uniquely interesting and unusual plant and one never tires of examining the curious flowers in minutest detail. The exquisite manner in which they have been fashioned by Nature almost defies description.

With all this, *P. caerulea* does best in a poor, stony soil and is a vigorous and rampant growing climber. A plant on our cottage wall, put in only eighteen months ago, has reached practically to roof level in this, its second season, while the half dozen blooms of its first summer have increased more than tenfold this year.

The Trumpet vine. Other exciting climbers seen at their best on a south or west wall include the trumpet vine, *Campsis grandiflora* (syn. *C. chinensis* and sometimes still known as *Bignonia* or *Tecoma*), which reaches a height of 20 feet and bears clusters of striking orange and red flowers in late summer and early autumn. It requires some support, but the North American form, *C. radicans*, is completely self-clinging, supporting itself, like the ivies, by means of aerial roots. The best variety to grow is Madame Gallen with salmon-red flowers.

Other relatively tender climbers that can be depended on to survive any but the severest winter when they are grown on sheltered walls are the unusual *Muehlenbeckia varians*, grown mainly for the curious beauty of its wiry interlaced stems and strangely shaped leaves, *Tecomaria capensis*, the Cape Honeysuckle, with brilliant pillar-box red trumpets, and *Trachelospermum jasminoides* whose fragrant jasmine-like flowers appear in July and August. The outstanding form of this last named twining shrub is *wilsonii*, one of E. H. Wilson's Chinese introductions, with leaves that vary in shape from lanceolate to oval and colour brilliantly in autumn.

Wall Shrubs

It is, however, not only the climbers proper that appreciate the support and protection of a wall. By widening the beds at their feet we can offer sanctuary to many other delicate shrubs which would not stand up to the vagaries of our winter climate in more exposed positions.

Abutilon. *Abutilon megapotamicum* is one of these, with foliage that is hop-like in appearance and elegant pendent flowers whose red calyces, yellow petals and brown anthers give the appearance of a colourful *corps de ballet* in action. There is a form with variegated foliage, whose yellow and green leaves have such similar symptoms to an advanced case of virus infection that I have never liked to grow it in my garden.

Ceanothus. Many of the ceanothuses are safest when grown against a south or west wall. In general the evergreen species and hybrids are more tender than the deciduous forms. Thus the evergreen *Ceanothus burkwoodii*, Delight, Cascade, A. T. Johnson and *veitchianus* all with flowers of various shades of intense blue, will benefit from the protection afforded in these situations.

Pomegranate. Even the pomegranate, *Punica granatum*, with its exotic-sounding name and sub-tropical associations, is perfectly hardy on a sunny south wall in milder parts of Britain.

Other shrubs. South America has sent us many exciting and colourful shrubs, including the brilliant Chilean Firebush, *Embothrium coccineum lanceolatum*, a lime-hater hardy in most parts of the country. There are few, however, that can compare with the more tender *Tricuspidaria lanceolata*, another lime-hater more correctly but less often known as *Crinodendron hookerianum*. This is a compact wall shrub of moderate size suitable for mild districts and sheltered situations. Anyone seing it in May, when its branches are thickly hung with glowing crimson lanterns, would agree that this is a plant that should find a place in any connoisseur's collection. Two of the kitchen shrubs, sweet bay and rosemary, which are equally valuable as garden plants, will both be safer against a sheltering wall, as also will that other outstanding shrub with aromatic foliage, the lemon verbena, *Lippia citriodora*.

Trees and Shrubs of Upright Habit

Another easy way of saving space is to include in your planting plan a number of plants of upright or columnar habit. Many of the better-known trees, shrubs and conifers have fastigiate forms, from the slender pillars of the flagpole cherry, *Prunus lannesiana* 'Erecta' or 'Amanogawa' to the pencil-slim 50-foot columns of the incense cedar, *Libocedrus decurrens*.

Such plants, however, must be used with discretion. Too many could have a dwarfing effect on the rest of the growing material and subjects must be chosen whose height is proportionate to the size of the garden. It would be unwise, for example, to plant a specimen of the Dawyck beech, *Fagus sylvatica* 'Fastigiata', in a small garden, because although its lateral spread does not exceed 10 to 12 feet, it will eventually tower 50 feet or more above the house and garden.

The Irish yew. Many of the fastigiate conifers, however, are of dimensions more appropriate to the average-sized garden. The erect Irish Yew, *Taxus baccata* 'Fastigiata', for example, grows only 12 to 15 feet tall and a place could be found for one or more in even the smallest of gardens. It is particularly effective planted with flowering shrubs. Its dark green foliage, looking almost black by contrast, makes an effective foil to the lighter green leaves and colourful blossoms of the latter.

Cypresses. Many of the cypresses are columnar in habit. Varieties of Lawson's Cypress such as *Chamaecyparis lawsoniana* 'Allumii', 'Fletcheri' and *lutea*, for example, form dense upright pyramids of grey-green, glaucous blue, blue-grey and gold, respectively. Two of my particular favourites are Jackman's form of *C. l.* 'Erecta', in which the foliage is presented in vertical slices, edge on to give a most unusual layered effect, together with *C. l.* 'Columnaris', which makes a dense narrow column of glaucous blue.

Juniper. The Irish juniper, *Juniperus communis hibernica*, like its compatriot the Irish yew, makes a slender pillar of great charm, although as it grows older it may require a girdle or two to prevent middle-aged spread of its branches. It has a miniature counterpart in *J. communis* 'Compressa', which, growing only 2 feet tall, makes an ideal focal plant in a group of dwarf shrubs or in a planting of heaths or alpines.

Successional Planting

Another way of increasing the capacity of the small garden is the obvious though often overlooked one of making more use of the available space. The herbaceous border affords a good example of how this can be accomplished. In the normal way, it is a feature that begins to make an impact from the middle of June onwards with the peak period coming in July and August. In many gardens it represents practically wasted space for seven months of the year.

Early-flowering plants. We can extend the display period considerably by the inclusion of earlier flowering perennials like the Leopardsbane (*Doronicum plantagineum*), lungworts, pulsatilla, hepatica, anchusa, the giant forget-me-not (*Brunnera macrophylla*, also known as *Anchusa myosotidiflora*), *Dryas octopetala*, the Globe Flower (*Trollius*), bearded irises, peonies, oriental poppies, Solomon's seal (*Polygonatum multiflorum*), together with bulbous plants like the spring snowflake (*Leucojum vernum*), scillas, chionodoxas, cultivated bluebells and, of course, groups of daffodils and narcissus.

Pairing off. Another way of prolonging the display in the herbaceous border is to adopt a horticultural system of pairing off, to provide replacements for the plants that give the early display. Broadly speaking, these consist of lupins, delphiniums, peonies, oriental poppies, irises, anchusa and aquilegia.

By the time their flowering season is over, many of these are looking shabby, and when the main display has passed its peak something will be needed to take their place, or the appearance of the border in autumn will be marred by areas of dead and decaying foliage.

This is not, of course, so noticeable when the garden is large and the border can be sited well away from the house. But where it forms an integral part of a small garden plan, something must be done to prevent it from becoming what might almost be described as an eyesore.

Pairing off consists of providing a group of late-flowering perennials for each early one that goes over. In this way, the colour gaps are soon filled again by fresh reinforcements of blossom as summer moves into early autumn.

Careful planning, however, is necessary to ensure that the subjects chosen will live harmoniously together. In spite of what is written to the contrary, lupins and delphiniums, in my opinion, need a complete rest after their magnificent early summer display. The second crop of flowers that is obtained by cutting them down in June and feeding them intensively does not warrant the strain on the plants that is incurred. Consequently, I find it better to plan for a second rhapsody in blue by planting the stately *Salvia uliginosa*, whose azure flower spikes start to appear in September and carry on until the frosts cut them down. This combination will lead to a peaceful co-existence for several years before dividing and replanting is necessary.

Irises. I sometimes wonder, as I watch their brief but breathtaking display, why I grow irises in the border at all. And yet the June border would scarcely seem complete without them and I would not willingly forego such gems as the translucent flesh-coloured Powder Pink, the salmon-pink Spindrift or the striking orange Arab Chief, to name only three outstanding irises, just because their flowering season is limited to a few short weeks.

Golden rod. The iris foliage soon becomes dilapidated though, the green swords turn brown and there is very little fresh growth to replace them. These faded charms can soon be camouflaged by some of the smaller and less vigorous varieties of Michaelmas daisy or golden rod (*Solidago*). The newer forms of this last-named plant are no longer the menace that their predecessors were. Two-foot-tall varieties, such as Goldenmosa or Leraft, both bearing mimosa-like sprays of blossom, or the more compact Lemore or Tom Thumb, form smaller clumps that do not invade neighbouring territory in the way that the older ones did. They can safely be planted behind the irises – but not in among them, since the iris rhizomes like to be sun-baked in summer – in which position they will continue the colour cavalcade during August and September.

Michaelmas daisies. Alternatively, if you prefer the longer and later display provided by the perennial asters, the *novi-belgii* section will provide just what is needed. The beetroot-red Winston S. Churchill ($2\frac{1}{2}$ feet) or violet-blue, late-flowering, frost-resistant Jean (2 feet), are both well-suited for the purpose, but best of all, perhaps, are some of the foot-high dwarfs such as the delicate pink Margaret Rose or the slower-growing pink Rosebud. Snowsprite, too, with its large white flowers, makes an excellent plant for the front of the border.

Rudbeckias. Oriental poppies flaunt their handsome blossoms throughout the month of June and afterwards subside into a tangle of sprawling stems and shabby foliage. *Rudbeckia speciosa*, better known perhaps as Black-eyed Susan, will soon distract the eye from this distressing sight with its close-packed foliage and orange-yellow, black-centred daisy blooms. *R. sullivanti* 'Goldsturm' is a variety with larger flowers and longer stems that is rapidly gaining in popularity, and will serve a similar purpose.

These are just a few of the combinations that could prove satisfactory. A study of nursery catalogues, with particular attention to height and flowering season, will suggest many more. Two other examples that come to mind are peonies, followed by nerines, and anchusa or aquilegias giving place to the succulent foliage and pink, flat-topped blossoms of the ice plant, *Sedum spectabile*.

Chapter Six

Space Savers

In previous chapters I have discussed ways and means by which available space can be used to best advantage. With the really small garden, however, it may be necessary to use a somewhat different approach. With the gardens of new houses shrinking all the time as land speculators cram quart-size houses into pint-sized plots, one solution would seem to be the use of miniature and dwarf forms of shrubs and conifers already known to us in their more orthodox guise.

Choosing dwarf shrubs. If you look through a nursery catalogue, you will find that certain species and varieties of shrubs are followed by the Latin suffixes 'Pygmaea', 'Nana', 'Minima', 'Compressa', or 'Compacta'. All of these indicate that the subjects in question are dwarf or compact forms which, in the majority of instances, are almost perfect replicas, in miniature, of their taller and better known counterparts.

Such shrubs and conifers provide ideal planting material for the owner of the really small garden, who is keen to make the very most of his limited space to grow as wide a variety of plants as possible. By a judicious selection of these delightful dwarfs he will be able to pack as many as a dozen or so into the space occupied by one shrub of normal dimensions.

Miniature roses. Most of the popular shrub groups contain these dwarf forms, including the rose family which is noteworthy for the fascinating miniatures that are enjoying such great popularity at the present time. Even a window-box will accommodate a half-dozen or more of the tiniest of these roses in miniature whose ultimate height and spread will not exceed 12 inches.

Many of them are named varieties of the old China Rose, *Rosa chinensis*, and include mini-roses like Humpty Dumpty, with double carmine pink blossoms, Tinker Bell, a deep pink double dwarf, Cinderella, a carmine-tinted white and, the tiniest of them all, a minute pink rose named *R. roulettii* (syn. *R. chinensis* 'Minima'), which grows only 6 inches tall and is thus ideally suited for window-box, rock or sink garden. Of less midget dimensions but still stopping short at $2\frac{1}{2}$ feet are a number of charming in-betweens that include Baby Masquerade, a perfect miniature of its well-known multi-coloured taller relation, Bit o' Sunshine, a bright yellow rose with shapely pointed buds, Maid Marion (syn. Mon Trésor), a deep red, and Oakington Ruby, with bright red flowers and a semi-prostrate habit of growth.

By careful selection, it would be possible to plan an entire rose garden in miniature, by planting the very dwarf forms at the edge and using the taller miniatures for background planting. Not everyone, however, and I suspect that I am in agreement with them, would be particularly enamoured of the rather precious effect of a feature such as this, and many of us would probably prefer to grow a limited number of roses of more orthodox habit and proportions.

But there is nothing precious or *outré* about the appearance of dwarf and miniature shrubs and conifers. They have a character all their own and many, albeit *very* slowly, will eventually reach heights approaching 6 feet, often, however, taking twice that number of years to do so.

Buying miniature shrubs. Just a word or two of warning, however, to those who contemplate ordering these pygmy shrubs 'sight unseen', so to speak, from catalogues. Because of their minute size and slow rate of growth, specimens sent out by nurseries are of necessity very small indeed although the plants may be actually five years old. Brace yourself for a shock, therefore, when that miniature shrub with the outsize botanical name, for which you have paid quite an appreciable sum of money, turns out to be a tiny scrap of root and top growth only a few inches tall. If you will stop to compare the proportionate rate of growth of these miniatures with that of the forms of normal size, you will realize that this must be the case. This is even more apparent where dwarf conifers are concerned, and although many dwarf evergreens and deciduous shrubs have a more rapid rate of growth and spread, it must be admitted that gardening with these miniature forms can be quite a costly hobby. But the returns and rewards warrant the initial outlay. By making use of them in the really small garden we can create a perfect Lilliputian version of the garden of more orthodox size, in which we must shrink ourselves to Alice-in-Wonderland dimensions to appreciate their pygmy proportions to the full.

Many species of berberis and cotoneaster have varieties of miniature habit. These include a number that are evergreen and should provide an excellent framework for the kind of feature that we have in mind.

Dwarf barberries. I particularly like *Berberis irwinii* 'Corollina compacta' (sometimes listed as 'Nana'), not only for the distinctive beauty of its coral-tinted flower buds which, when they open, smother the branches in deep orange flowers, but also for the neat appearance of the close-packed olive green foliage. Another good evergreen form is *B. buxifolia nana*, with a more rounded habit of growth and dark-green leaves that turn purplish in winter. The pendent flowers of this variety, which are amber-coloured, appear somewhat earlier than those of most others – towards the end of March. Both grow to a height of about $2\frac{1}{2}$ to 3 feet.

One of the finest shrubs of any for brilliance of leaf colour is *B. thunbergii* 'Atropurpurea', a deciduous barberry whose leaves, bronzy-red throughout spring and summer, assume even more vivid scarlet tints before they fall. These sterling qualities are shared by the miniature variety 'Atropurpurea Nana', which grows only 2 feet tall with a spread of the same dimensions. In all but the most restricted space I would plant in groups of three or more, so that the full impact of this brilliant display of leaf colour can be fully enjoyed.

Cotoneasters. Among the dwarf and miniature cotoneasters are several which, although less than a foot tall, have a very extensive lateral spread. This need not deter us from using them in a restricted space. If they are kept in check by pruning they will soon form ground-hugging hummocks, whose evergreen foliage and bright autumn berries make them extremely useful either as edging plants or ground cover.

One of the most attractive is *Cotoneaster congestus*, also found listed as *pyrenaicus*. This diminutive species has very small leaves that form a close-packed cushion $1\frac{1}{2}$ to 2 feet in height. *C. dammeri* is a prostrate form and although it grows only a few inches tall it will spread over a disproportionately wide area, if left to grow unchecked. I find it a useful ground cover plant which looks very effective overspilling a brick or paved path. Its bright red berries and evergreen foliage make this an outstandingly useful dwarf shrub.

The fishbone cotoneaster, *C. horizontalis*, with a more vigorous habit of growth, can be utilized in a similar manner where more space is available. In the small garden, however, it will be found most useful for covering low walls and it looks particularly well on bungalow walls, where more rampant and taller growing wall shrubs would be out of keeping. This good-tempered plant, much beloved by the bees when the small, pink-tinged, white blossoms open in early May, is deciduous, but this is no disadvantage as it enables us to appreciate more thoroughly the herringbone pattern of the branches that gives it its name, thickly studded with bright red boot-button berries. It is indifferent to aspect and is one of the few berried shrubs that will fruit almost as well on a north wall as on any other.

There is also a variegated form, 'Variegatus', which is not often seen, with a more prostrate habit than that of the type. The grey leaves are margined with silver and develop attractive crimson tints before they fall in autumn.

Two other species that will provide an evergreen carpet under low-growing shrubs or will look well in borders where space is restricted are *C. prostratus*, with closely-packed foliage lavishly studded with red autumn berries, and *C. salicifolius* 'Autumn Fire', which has striking willow-like leaves and bears its scarlet berries in clusters in the same way that many of the larger species and varieties do.

A dwarf buddleia. Most varieties of *Buddleia davidii* are too space-consuming for the really small garden but there is one that anyone who loves the sight of the tasselled flowers covered in brilliant butterflies ought to find the room for. This is the compact *B. d. nanhoensis*, a dainty and elegant form that grows only 5 or 6 feet tall and can be kept even more restricted by severe annual pruning in March. The colour of the flower spikes is not as exciting as that of Royal Red, Black Knight or some of the newer, but taller introductions, but they offer just as irresistible an attraction to the Red Admirals and Peacocks that flock to them in dozens on bright sunny days.

Cytisus. There are a few dwarf and miniature brooms that are just as attractive, whether in flower or out, as their taller, more leggy relations. Probably the best known and most widely grown of these is *Cytisus kewensis*, with sulphur yellow flowers borne on supple arching twigs that seldom exceed a foot in height. Although most commonly grown in the rock garden, the elegant architectural form of this broom would be of the utmost value in a border devoted to small shrubs. Two others of prostrate habit, both bearing flowers of a brighter yellow, are *C. ardoinii* and *C. procumbens*, both of which are true dwarfs. The former has a restricted spread, but *C. procumbens* will wander much farther afield, covering an area of 6 feet or more if allowed to spread unchecked.

Genistas. The genistas also provide us with several miniature forms of great beauty. *G. tinctoria* 'Plena', a double form of the dyer's greenweed, bears a profusion of double yellow flowers on 9-inch stems; the better known *G. lydia*, $2\frac{1}{2}$ to 3 feet tall, has curved shoots clustered with gold. Flowering, as they do, in late May and throughout most of June, the genistas make a good follow-on to the earlier blooming cytisus species.

Mock oranges. A border of miniature shrubs need not lack for fragrance in summer. Several small forms of the Mock Orange, *Philadelphus*, will provide it in just as generous a measure as their taller cousins. The philadelphus are first-rate garden shrubs that make an excellent showing on even the poorest of soils. To get the best results from them, the flowering shoots, together with any unwanted growth, should be cut out after the blossoms have faded. The Mock Oranges flower on the new season's growth and this practice will keep the plants shapely and prevent them from getting leggy.

Manteau d'Hermine is an enchanting dwarf bearing its double white flowers in abundance. Sybille's flowers are distinguished by a centre blotch of purple. Its habit of growth is more arching, although neither of these grows taller than about 4 feet. *P. microphyllus*, a small-leaved species, gets slightly taller, and makes a wiry, twiggy plant whose architectural form is attractive. The single flowers have a particularly rich fragrance.

Rhododendrons. The owner of the small garden with lime-free soil and conditions of partial shade has a wide range of dwarf and compact rhododendrons from which he can choose a small collection. I grow these attractive miniatures in a bed of modest proportions that slopes down to a rill of water and enjoys the dappled shade of a nearby oak. They suit their situation to perfection, since to have grown taller subjects in this position would have not only thrown the planting out of proportion, but would also have dwarfed the tiny stream to insignificance.

It was not until I had been growing it for several years that I woke up to the fact that the widely-grown bright red rhododendron Britannia is a semi-dwarf. Although I ought to have known better, I was puzzled to know why it was lagging so far behind its neighbours. When I found out I used it as the nucleus of my waterside planting. At its present height of 3 feet, it towers over most of the others, but this disparity of height gives that much-desired variety of interest.

Among the dwarf rhododendron species, *R. racemosum* and *R. radicans* are both well worth growing. They would make excellent subjects for the middle and edges of the miniature shrub border. My own specimens, newly planted last year, are interplanted with epimediums which will fill the gaps until the rhododendrons reach maturity. *R. racemosum* makes a dense plant, 3 to 4 feet in height – this after quite a number of years – with round leathery leaves and attractive pink double flowers. 'Forrest's Dwarf' is a form which would do well in the front row of the rhododendron chorus. *R. radicans* itself is a prostrate alpine species that would be very much at home on the northerly slopes of the rock garden but looks just as attractive carpeting a shady bed. The purple flowers are large for such a dwarf plant, being almost an inch in diameter.

Many growers consider *R. yakusimanum*, which is a relatively new introduction, to be the finest of all the smaller rhododendrons. This judgement is well deserved, since 'Yak', as it is familiarly called, is as noteworthy for the beauty of its pale pink flower trusses as for the attractive appearance of the silver-felted young leaves when they unfurl in June. It grows to a height of about three feet.

'Carmen' is even more compact and low-growing, with magnificent dark red blooms as exotic as its name. *R. impeditum* makes a bushy plant massed in May with violet flowers; *R. williamsianum*, another with a low and spreading habit, has additional attractions to its soft pink flowers in fine heart-shaped leaves and bronzy young shoots.

In complete colour contrast to all these is the somewhat taller Yellow Hammer, which bears its bright yellow tubular flowers in pairs. This is in the same tradition as many of the larger yellow species and hybrids. Yellow, to my mind, is the most beautiful of all rhododendron colours. It appears again in the lesser known *R. keiskei*, whose flowers are a soft creamy yellow, of a less brilliant shade than those of Yellow Hammer.

Pink is well represented in other dwarf forms besides *racemosum*. These include *R. hirsutum* 'Flore Pleno' with double tubular flowers, *R. kotschyi* (syn. *R. ferrugineum myrtifolium*), which bears generous clusters of pink blossom, and Temple Belle, a compact five-footer whose campanulate flowers are a lovely translucent pink.

Whites, on the other hand are comparatively rare. One of the most attractive is *R. microleucum* which makes a tiny but dense shrub with grey-green foliage that is thickly spattered with dainty white flowers in April and May.

Quite the most dazzling of any, however, is Elizabeth, a cross between *R. griersonianum* and *R. repens*, whose flower clusters are a dazzling orange-red.

These smaller rhododendrons are valuable as much for the

In a Berkshire garden

Two varieties of *Camellia x williamsii*. (*Above*) 'Donation' and (*below*) 'J. C. Williams'

(*Above*) *Hybiscus syriacus* 'Blue Bird'; (*below*) the witch hazel
Hamamellis mollis

Two hellebores. (*Above*) *Helleborus corsicus* and (*below*) *H. niger*

(Above) Clematis montana; *(below) Vitis coignetiae*

Two brooms. (*Above*) *Spartium junceum* and (*below*) *Cytisus praecox*

(*Above*) the Scotch thistle *Onopordon acanthium*; (*below*) a grouping of hostas and gunnera in the author's garden

(*Above*) the large-leaved *Hosta sieboldiana*; (*below*) *H. fortunei* 'Albo-picta' in its yellow spring dress

Hostas in shady corners

Two ivies. (*Above*) *Hedera canariensis* and (*below*) the gold-
leaved *H. colchica dentata* 'Variegatum'

(*Above left*) *Molucella laevis* ('Bells of Ireland'). (*Above right*) the sea-holly *Eryngium alpinum*

(*Below left*) *Fatshedera lizei*. (*Below right*) the ornamental grass, *Glyceria aquatica* 'Variegata'

(*Above*) *Rhododendron* 'Pink Pearl' *and* (*below*) *R.* 'Loderi'

(*Above*) *Rhododendron* 'Mrs. G. W. Leak'
(*Below*) *R. williamsianum*

(*Left*)
Yucca filamentosa

(*Below*)
A small garden in
Warwickshire

(*Above*) Some trough gardens; (*below*) *Dictamnus albus*

Gunnera manicata

continuing interest of their evergreen foliage in winter and summer alike, as for the decorative quality of their flowers and their ability to bring brilliant colour to the shadier parts of the garden.

Given suitable soil conditions and the requisite partial shade, they are among the best garden all-rounders of any shrubs, and this is particularly true of the dwarfs and miniatures, whose compact and tidy habit of growth and almost complete freedom from pests and diseases make them ideal plants for the gardener whose space and time for the pursuit of his hobby are restricted.

DWARF CONIFERS

But it is not only rhododendrons and other evergreen shrubs that possess these sterling qualities. Many dwarf conifers, perfect miniature replicas of their taller prototypes, share them to a marked degree and deserve representation in any garden that aspires to creating an atmosphere combining year-long interest with the maximum variety of plantings.

Dwarf conifers represent, however, even more than the subjects already mentioned, a long-term policy, since they are a very long time a'growing. Many may take ten years or longer to reach maturity. There are, however, so many attractive and unusual forms that the results are well worth waiting for. At Grayswood Hill, near Haslemere, Mr G. L. Pilkington has one of the finest and most comprehensive collections of dwarf conifers in the country. No matter what time of year you visit his garden, these, for me at any rate, always steal the limelight from the brilliant and carefully contrived displays in other parts of the garden.

Dwarf cypresses. Most of us are familiar with the popular Lawson's Cypress in its many lovely and unusual varieties. The species includes many delightful dwarfs with the typical broad-based pyramidal habit of their larger relations. *Chamaecyparis lawsoniana nana*, for example, slowly develops into a solid-looking cone of rich green foliage. *C. l.* 'Minima', an even more compact form, has vertical main stems, with side branchlets that are set at right angles to give an edge-on view of the foliage that is singularly attractive. There is also a fine golden variety, 'Minima Aurea', as well as one with blue-grey foliage, *minima glauca*.

Others differ greatly in character from the orthodox conical shape. *C. l.* 'Nidiformis', a cross between *C. lawsoniana* and *C. nootkatensis*, has bluish-green foliage and arching spread. *C. obtusa* 'Nana Aurea' (*C. obtusa* 'Pygmaea') is a flat-topped form with fan-shaped foliage that is bronze-tipped in winter.

The *pisifera* species that used to be known as *Retinospora* have a more feathery type of foliage, particularly at their immature stage of growth. The names are very long for such compact little gems, but unfortunately there is no other way of identifying them. *C. pisifera* 'Compacta variegata', for example, makes a dense little mound that my favourite nurseryman very aptly describes as 'bun-shaped'; its foliage is flecked with gold. Another of similar habit is *C. p.* 'Plumosa Compressa' which likes partial shade and forms a tight little half sphere – another way of calling it bun-shaped – of soft green foliage speckled with gold.

Junipers. The junipers, too, include in their extensive ranks one outstandingly attractive miniature species whose slender columns make first-rate focal plants in a mixed planting of dwarf shrubs. This is *Juniperus communis* 'Compressa', whose blue-grey pencil-slim pillars seldom exceed 24 inches in height. It is extremely slow-growing and is a dwarf form of the common juniper, which is one of our three native conifers. The partiality of the latter for the chalk downs of our southern counties explains why all the junipers benefit from occasional dressings of carbonate of lime.

Dwarf spruce and pine. One of the most fascinating of these pygmy conifers is a member of the Christmas Tree family, a dwarf spruce known as *Picea abies* 'Nidiformis'; a spreading mass of closely needled, crowded branches with a flat top, looking remarkably like a birds' nest, which accounts for this conifer's Latin suffix. Or perhaps your preference would be for a dwarf Scots Pine, perfect in every detail, but only 4 or 5 feet tall. *Pinus sylvestris* 'Beauvronensis' will fill the bill, with its short branches, closely packed with needles of a greenish-blue.

A small yew. Although the more common forms of yew are relatively slow-growing, established plants can reach quite sizeable proportions in 10 years or so. This, however, is not the case with the upright form, *Taxus baccata* 'Fastigiata Standishii', which makes an ideal subject for a lawn specimen or for a formal paved garden or terrace. It would also give an air of distinction to a small front garden, making a slim golden column that stops growing when it reaches a height of about 5 or 6 feet.

Although these miniature shrubs and conifers have been discussed in the context of really restricted garden space, they can be equally useful and attractive in the larger garden. Collecting them can be a fascinating if somewhat expensive garden pursuit, or for those who want only a few, individual specimens can make effective contrast plants in the rock or heath garden.

First and foremost, however, they provide a ready solution to the problems of the owner of the pocket-handkerchief plot who wants to grow out-of-the-ordinary plants in as great a variety as possible.

Chapter Seven

You, too, can Specialize

Whenever I talk to people about gardening, they usually ask me, before long, 'What do you specialize in ?' I always have to answer, a trifle shamefacedly, 'Nothing.' The truth is, I am temperamentally unsuited to this kind of gardening, much as I admire those who engage in it. I take off my hat to the man who spends the greater part of his gardening life mating reluctant rhododendrons or arranging marriages of convenience between camellias, but this, I fear, is not my kind of gardening.

There are too many lovely and varied plants to grow for me to be able to concentrate my entire time and interest on just one or two groups. And yet, I suppose I do specialize to a degree and, in doing so, bring to my gardening a fuller interest, gaining in return an added satisfaction. And anyone, no matter how small their garden, can do the same, and earn the right to call themselves, perhaps not out-and-out specialists, but at least connoisseurs or collectors.

Certain plant groups or species lend themselves much more freely to this pursuit than others, and once you have been bitten by the collecting bug, it is surprising what a fillip it can give to your enjoyment of gardening.

In a modest way, my wife and I between us collect camellias, peonies, irises, hostas, hellebores and rhododendron species. At present I am engaged in acquiring a representative collection of viburnums, but of this more later.

These are only a few of the genera that lend themselves to this hobby. On a more modest scale there are such things as sweet peas, chrysanthemums, dahlias, day lilies or michaelmas daisies, or on a lesser scale still, alpines, heaths, succulents or rock roses. A collection of any of these can be housed in a very restricted space. Even a sink garden or window-box can contain a collection of sempervivums, of which the common houseleek is probably the best-known example.

For a start, however, let us talk about some of the more garden-worthy plants that make suitable subjects for the average amateur. In general, these should not only be relatively easy to grow but also easy to obtain in commerce. In addition, they should not be too demanding as to soil conditions.

The suggestions that follow have a strong personal bias, but any gardener worthy of the name will be able to make his own choice before setting up as a plant specialist on his own account.

Hellebores

To many of us the name hellebore means only one plant, the lovely Christmas rose, *Helleborus niger*. That was what I used to think, too, until the lady of the garden started to go in for flower arrangement in a big way. The quest for suitable flowers and foliage for her demonstrations resulted in the introduction of a whole new range of plants in the garden. Among them were various hitherto unfamiliar species and varieties of hellebore, which are greatly in demand for winter and early spring arrangements because of the subtle muted greens, pinks and purples of their attractive flowers.

The Christmas rose itself, which, incidentally, in our part of the country, the Surrey-Sussex borders, needs assistance from cloches or cold frames if it is to live up to its name, is too well known to need description. In the past few years it has been rapidly gaining popularity as a florist's flower, particularly at the Christmas season. This is not surprising. Its pure white chalices and golden stamens have a purity of line and form that evokes the very spirit of Christmastide. No wonder, too, that it is becoming almost as popular a feature of Christmas card illustration as the ubiquitous robin and holly.

Next to *H. niger*, the species most commonly grown is the Lenten rose, *H. orientalis*. This hails from Greece and Asia Minor and there are several first-rate garden forms. The palmate leaves are more finely divided than those of the Christmas rose and are held more erectly on longer stems. The flowers – two or three to a stem – vary in colour a great deal. Some are cream, others green, while the majority range from a light puce-pink to a deep blackish-purple.

As its name suggests, the flowers of the Lenten rose do not appear until late February. They continue throughout March and April and will still be looking attractive until the end of May.

Helleborus foetidus, the setterwort, or less politely named stinking hellebore, is a native of this country. It earns its derogatory title on account of the unpleasant scent of its green flowers. It comes into bloom early in February and bears clusters of pale green blossoms, tipped with purple. One of the distinctive qualities of this species is its finely divided evergreen foliage. The leaves, which are narrow and strap-like with a slightly serrated edge, have a deep central rib.

Helleborus foetidus is one of the taller species, growing to a height of 2 feet or more. It has a long flowering season that lasts from February until May.

Helleborus viridis is another green-flowered species that is also a native of these isles, being found in the wild in some parts of Ireland. The flowers are a pale apple green that contrasts strikingly with the darker green of the foliage. We seldom see the purple Caucasian species, *H. abchasicus* although it should be more widely grown for, flowering as it does in early January, it makes a good follow-up for the Christmas Rose. There are two interesting varieties, 'Coccineus', whose flowers are wine-red in colour, and 'Venosus' whose flowers are etched with a darker veining.

My own favourite among the hellebores is the Corsican variety, which was formerly known as *H. corsicus* and which I believe we now have to call *H. lividus corsicus*. This is an outstandingly handsome plant, growing 3 feet tall. The flowers are borne on tall, erect stems in large clusters, with as many as twenty to a spike. Their green is the green of young peapods while the leaves are large and fleshy, veined like morocco leather and with deeply toothed edges.

This attractive variety comes into flower in March and continues to bloom throughout April. An amazing feature of this plant is the way that the flowers persist, remaining attractive until August. No wonder the flower arrangers, with their passion for green blooms, are going into raptures over this lovely species.

Cultivation. Once established, hellebores resent disturbance. Their requirements are simple; well-drained soil and a modicum of shade, with regular dressings of peat or leafmould.

As they are to remain permanently in one place, careful initial preparation of the planting positions will pay subsequent dividends. If the soil is heavy, plenty of well-rotted compost or stable manure should be incorporated in the first and second spits, while a few buckets of sharp sand or grit will help to provide the open texture that they prefer.

Irises

Although I am firmly 'hooked' myself, I sometimes wonder that so many gardeners find themselves with an incurable addiction to the tall bearded irises. They have a very short flowering season and although the sword-like foliage is tidy, it is not exactly outstanding, particularly if it falls a victim, as it so often does, to fungus disease in wet summers. And yet the iris has a tremendous following, both here and in the USA.

Its popularity, I suppose, must be due, in no small measure, to the perfect form of its heraldic blossoms, the fleur-de-lis of former times, as much as to their wide and attractive colour range. Almost every colour in the spectrum is represented and the only ones that are missing – so far – are the more brilliant shades of scarlet.

You can pay a king's ransom for new introductions but there are plenty of outstanding named varieties which have stood the test of time and are obtainable for a few shillings. Those that follow are varieties that I have grown and found satisfactory.

Selected varieties. Of the self-coloured blues, I like the following: Aline, azure, Blue Ensign, a rich violet-blue, Elmohr, one of the 'good old good ones' from the USA with outsize mulberry flowers, and Salisbury, a restrained ice-blue.

I have grown many yellows but of them all I still prefer Mabel Chadburn, the richest golden-yellow self. Golden Hind, a clear chrome yellow, runs it a close second for popularity. Arab Chief, with flowers of a lambent orange-buff strikes a more exotic note.

Until fairly recently, pink irises were a rarity and plants were astronomically expensive. Today they are more common and prices have fallen to more reasonable levels. Of the pinks, one of my favourites is Powder Pink, a lovely flesh-pink iris with falls of a lighter colour and a contrasting tangerine beard. Sweet Seventeen is a richer apricot-pink with a patch of lighter colour on the falls. Pink Cameo, an award-winning variety, is an exquisite flamingo pink while Pink Ruffles is a lovely frilled type of less vigorous growth than most, whose orchid-pink flowers are borne in great profusion. Still comparatively expensive at the time of writing is the fine raspberry-pink Mary Randall, the result of crossing and re-crossing the flamingo-pink varieties.

When we come to mixed colours the permutations and variations available are legion. You can take your choice from Brown Trout, with copper standards and red falls, City of Lincoln, an award-winning iris with bright golden standards and velvety red falls, and the newer and still relatively expensive Elizabeth Arden, well-named for its associations with beauty. The standards of this lovely variety are apricot-pink with cream falls. The colour blends of Melodist are striking and unusual in henna-red and rich apricot.

There are some lovely whites among the bearded irises as well as some midnight blues and deep purples that are almost dark enough to be considered as black. Cliffs of Dover is one of the best-known and most satisfactory whites. It is a tall iris with ruffled flowers of milky white, which has earned awards not only in the USA, its country of origin, but also from the Royal Horticultural Society here. It was given its name as a compliment to Britain, when it was first introduced in 1953. New Snow and Polar Ice are two other good white varieties, the latter being a very strong grower and an early flowerer.

Black Forest is well-named, as also is Black Hills. Both of these are a dark inky black with beards to match. Those who like something more out-of-the-ordinary might like to try some of the plicatas, in which the whole flower is delicately and closely etched with veins of a contrasting colour. My Smoky is one of the most famous of these in which the white ground is heavily marked with deep purple. Finally, for the flower arrangers once more, there is the popular chartreuse green Cleo, whose satin-textured self-coloured flowers have the delightful fragrance that is a characteristic of many other bearded irises.

Miniature irises. Those with less space at their disposal might prefer to collect the delightful miniature irises, which look particularly well in the rock garden and even when in flower do not exceed 9 inches in height. Goldfinch and The Bride, golden-yellow and white respectively, are two firm favourites, while two other inexpensive varieties, *atroviolacea*, with flowers like a rich purple velvet, and *cyanea*, a more intense violet-blue, are both well worth growing.

Some of the newer varieties are very striking. Amber Queen is a newish amber-yellow variety, Happy Thought is a brilliant sulphur yellow self while Stylish is a distinctive self of vivid petunia with a contrasting blue beard.

Iris sibirica. If you have water in your garden (or even if you have not, since they thrive quite well in the border but do not look quite so much at home there) your interest will probably extend to *Iris sibirica* and its forms. These make very large clumps and their grassy foliage is very attractive. Unlike that of the bearded irises, it remains unblemished throughout the summer, after the plants have flowered in May and June. The flowers, which are borne in great profusion, are reminiscent of those of the bulbous irises, *I. reticulata*.

I grew my first batch of *I. sibirica* plants from a handful of seed saved from a collection in a friend's garden. They needed quite a bit of nursing, but they all flowered in the third year and I had a good selection of colours that included various shades of blue and one very good creamy-white.

Since then I have acquired some of the named varieties,

which of course are mostly hybrids between *I. sibirica* and *I. orientalis*, but I cannot say that many of them show any outstanding improvement on my seedlings. For those who want more rapid results, however, I can recommend Dragon Fly, with sky-blue flowers veined with black, Gatineau, a good clear blue and Eric the Red, a really striking variety with reddish-purple standards and falls, the latter being beautifully marked with yellow and white.

Other species. Recently, I have started to add some of the other species to my modest collection. *I. kaempferi*, which, alas, does not tolerate lime, is a very good species for damp places. The named varieties contain many glorious colours. Dark Cloud is a deep purple self, Dresden China is a lighter porcelain blue, while Galathea has white falls veined with violet and violet standards.

Iris laevigata is another moisture-lover; the variety *montrosa* has large and exotic-looking flowers resembling those of an orchid. They are inky blue with a white centre, the latter being slightly flecked with purple. The blue does not quite extend to the edges of the petals which leaves them with an irregular narrow margin of white.

Iris foetidissima is noteworthy in the main for the beauty of its glossy foliage and the bright scarlet berries that follow after the purple flowers. Another unusual iris that I have planted recently is the variety of *I. pallida* with green and silver striped foliage that my nurseryman tells me is in very short supply. Anyone who has the chance to get hold of a plant should snap it up at once.

The species mentioned here by no means exhaust the numbers available to the really enthusiastic collector. My gardening encyclopaedia lists more than fifty, so that anyone who wants to go in for collecting irises in a really big way will have plenty of scope for his efforts.

The winter iris. There is one pearl among irises that we must not forget whether we specialize or not. That is *Iris unguicularis* (*I. stylosa*), whose flowers have brought me more pleasure on dreary winter days than those of almost any other plant I have ever grown.

Give this iris a sheltered sun-baked position at the foot of a wall and poor soil (on heavy soils mix in plenty of brick or mortar rubble) and it will never fail to oblige with a continuous supply of scented sky-blue flowers from November right through until March. In addition to the type, there is a deeper lavender-blue form 'Superba', as well as a white one, but I have grown neither of these, having always been perfectly content with the ethereal beauty of the common form.

Herbaceous Peonies

I have mentioned the tree peonies on page 26 and here am concerned with herbaceous species. There can be few garden plants, and surely no perennials with greater all-round decorative qualities than this lovely race of plants. Beauty of blossom, long life, ease of cultivation and foliage of great interest, with all these virtues and fragrance thrown in for good measure, the peony is a border subject of sterling character.

History of peonies. It is a plant that can boast, in addition, a long and distinguished lineage. Peonies of the *officinalis* group were well known to the ancient Greeks who used their seeds, roots and leaves in medicine. It is mentioned in the writings of Pliny and Dioscorides. In the Middle Ages the roots were boiled and eaten as vegetables, while the seeds were ground up and used as seasoning.

Many oriental manuscripts, dating back as far as the seventh century AD, pay glowing tributes to its elegance and beauty. When it was subsequently introduced into Japan, its possession and cultivation were restricted to the Emperor and persons of noble birth, which probably makes it one of the earliest of all status symbols. Peonies have been grown in this country for more than 900 years, but although they appear frequently in the formal flower paintings of the seventeenth and eighteenth centuries, they did not come under the influence of the specialist plant breeders until the latter half of the nineteenth. Foremost among these was the Frenchman, Victor Lemoine of Nancy, whose nursery was responsible for the development and improvement of so many of our present-day shrubs. At this period, the Chinese peony, *Paeonia lactiflora* (also known as *P. albiflora*) was crossed with *P. wittmanniana* and *P. officinalis* to produce a host of striking new hybrids.

The plants that resulted fall into five main groups – singles, Japanese, anemone-flowered, semi-doubles and doubles. The singles have five or more outer petals surrounding a central boss of golden stamens. In the Japanese varieties these stamens have been modified into a cluster of sterile filaments like finely cut petals, that are known as staminodes. In the anemone-flowered kinds the stamens have undergone an even more radical transformation into a close group of narrow petals, or petaloid systems.

Cultivation. Peonies are very adaptable to varying conditions of sunshine or shade and will, in fact, grow quite satisfactorily under the light shade of fruit trees or small ornamental trees such as crabs and cherries.

There is one important planting rule that must always be observed if the plants are to flower with their typical generosity. The crowns of the plants must never be more than 2 inches below the surface of the soil; in heavy soils, in fact, 1 inch is sufficient.

Planting peonies too deeply is one of the main causes of disappointment. It results in sparse flowering, or even in no blossoms at all. If you stop to think that a mature plant can bear as many as twenty or thirty glorious blooms in a single season, it will be obvious how vitally important it is to remember this simple precaution. Peonies have a preference for heavy moist loam and will do well in either chalk or lime-free soils. Light soils can be rendered suitable by the addition of liberal quantities of leafmould or well-rotted compost. If stable manure is used, it should be buried well down in the second spit as it must not be allowed to come into contact with the roots of the plants. I prefer to use bonemeal, applied generously when the plants are first put in and forked in round them every second or third year afterwards.

Once the plants are in position, they should not be disturbed. More than any other herbaceous plant, they resent this. Left severely alone, they will increase in beauty and abundance of blossom with each succeeding year. Deep forking round them can cause damage to the thong-like roots, which are extremely brittle. It is better, therefore, to rely on mulches and hand weeding in the immediate vicinity of the plants.

Distances of between 3 and 4 feet between the plants should be sufficient for their full development, bearing in mind always that they can remain in the same position for twenty years or even longer.

By a careful choice of varieties it is possible to have peonies in flower for more than eight weeks in the year, from the last week in April to the first in July.

Selected peonies. Among the earliest to bloom are the varieties Othello and *P. whitleyi major* (also known as *P. alba grandiflora* and The Bride). These are both singles, cherry-red and white respectively. Early doubles include Edith Cavell, creamy-white with a yellowish tinge, and Wiesbaden, whose large coral pink blossoms are edged with white.

Since their nursery has played such an important role in the development of the modern peony, it is not surprising to find that the name of Kelway appears frequently in the nomenclature of many of the finest present-day varieties. Included in these are James Kelway, an exceptionally beautiful milk-white peony that enhances the perfection of its globular flowers with delicate fragrance, and Kelway's Glorious, which was chosen top peony of its year by the American Peony Society. This is a signal honour in a country that rates this group of plants so very highly.

Two fine pinks are represented by June Morning, a large delicate silvery-pink variety, and Kelway's Supreme, a blush pink variety that turns white as the flowers mature.

High-ranking among the best of the older doubles are the outstandingly beautiful Duchesse de Nemours, a free-flowering, delicately scented mid-season variety with elegant in-curved petals of yellow; Karl Rosenfeld, a fine example of the typical old crimson peony colour, and Sarah Bernhardt, an exquisite double pink whose petals are edged with silver. Festiva Maxima, which made its bow as long ago as 1851, is one of the oldest but still one of the loveliest of the doubles; its white flowers are unobtrusively flaked with crimson.

Of the less common forms, Madame Calot, an anemone-flowered variety, has an outer ring of pale pink petals and inner creamy-white petaloids. Globe of Light has guard petals of rose with yellow petaloids, while Reine Hortense, a pale pink splashed with crimson, makes an interesting complement to this.

The connoisseur will be interested in the various peony species that flower mainly during May. My first choice among these would be the one with the completely unpronounceable name, *Paeonia mlokosewitschii* which is a 'must' in any collection. It is in very short supply, and you sometimes have to wait for two years after ordering before you can obtain a plant, but the wait is, I promise you, well worth while. The globular flowers, of perfect form and symmetry are a lovely clear yellow, with golden stamens.

Another, which is grown as much for the decorative quality of its finely cut foliage as for the crimson flowers that usher in the peony parade in April, is *P. anomala*. The deep red dwarf variety, *P. tenuifolia plena*, makes a useful subject for the front of the border.

Rhododendron Species

Rhododendron species (by which is meant those that grow in the wild) make a good subject for the discerning collector who is also blessed with the requisite acid soil conditions. I go in for the giant-leaved species myself, but there are others to suit every taste and every size of garden, ranging from the miniature alpine species only a few inches tall, such as *R. pemakoense*, to the real giants of the *falconeri* series which, in suitable soils and situations, can reach heights of 25 feet and over – these are suitable only for the larger garden.

Many of these giant forms are of outstanding architectural and decorative value, out of flower as well as in. They would all be well worth growing for their foliage alone, the enormous flower trusses merely serving to set the seal on their distinctive qualities.

Site and soil. Until a few years ago I had never really had the suitable soil conditions so necessary for growing many of the wild species successfully. In addition to the acid soils that all rhododendrons demand, they also require plenty of moisture and partial shade during the summer months – a position under deciduous trees like silver birches and other light-foliaged trees with tall trunks suits them best.

Ever since I first cast covetous eyes on the magnificent specimens at Bodnant, I have always wanted to grow them.

I started to collect them in a modest way, beginning with a dozen or so of the better-known giants. Already the small specimens (I chose the smallest for economy's sake), about 18 inches to 2 feet in height and with incredibly large leaves, are adding considerably to the interest of what was formerly a rather dull rhododendron border, and are exciting the envy and admiration of many gardening friends.

Even gardeners, that admirable race of men, have been known to be guilty of practising one-upmanship and for those honest enough to confess to this failing, I can thoroughly recomment the large-leaved rhododendron species. With the leaves of some reaching lengths of 2 feet or more, there are few plants more capable of impressing the Joneses.

Selection of species. The first of the rhododendron species to reach this country was *R. hirsutum* which was introduced from Europe in the middle of the seventeenth century. Strangely enough *R. ponticum*, nowadays practically a native of our woods in many parts of the country, did not arrive until more than 100 years later. It was closely preceded by *R. ferrugineum*, the so-called Swiss Alpine Rose, a flat-topped hemispherical shrub, with pink flower trusses, which grows in limy soil.

The early years of the nineteenth century saw the introduction of the vigorous *R. catawbiense* from the eastern seaboard of the USA where, like *ponticum* in this country, it colonizes large stretches of woodland. This majestic species, which has played an important role in the parentage of many of the finest hybrids, was followed by a host of new arrivals from the Himalayas and the Far East, the first of the former being the well-known *R. arboreum*, which still makes a magnificent plant for gardens that can provide sufficient space for its proper development.

Rhododendron arboreum, as its name indicates, is tree-like in habit, with magnificent foliage, cream-felted on the reverse, and closely packed flower trusses, varying in different forms from white to deep red. This species is seen at its best in milder districts; it flourishes in Cornwall and western Scotland.

Throughout the 1800s and during the first thirty years of the present century, new rhododendron species continued to arrive in ever-increasing numbers. The tide reached full spate with the introductions of the famous collectors – Wilson, Forrest, Kingdon-Ward and others.

More than 750 species are listed in the rhododendron hand-book at the present time, and it is clear that the scope for the collector is very wide. The species described are, with only a few exceptions, those that I have enjoyed growing myself and now hope to grow with even greater success in the more suitable conditions of my new garden.

Although we seldom think of rhododendrons as foliage plants, the beauty of leaf form and texture in many of the larger species makes their leaves formidable rivals to the blossoms. The various species are divided up into Series and most of these big-leaved ones are found in the *falconeri* and *grande* Series. *R. falconeri* itself is probably the best-known and most widely grown of these. This stately rhododendron has been cultivated here for more than a century. With its deeply veined broad oval leaves, 6 inches in width, more than twice that length and cinammon-felted on their undersides, together with its enormous flower trusses, *R. falconeri* is in a class by itself.

It will need lots of *lebensraum* if it is to display its majestic proportions to the fullest effect, as well as a position in partial shade. If you are able to satisfy these requirements, have a sheltered garden and the requisite acid soil, *R. falconeri* should develop into a specimen 20 feet in height, with a spread of similar dimensions.

I have planted, as well, *R. basilicum*, another of the large-leaved species. I am told that it is more tender than *R. falconeri*, but plants are flourishing in a neighbouring garden, so I am hoping for success with it. It grows less rapidly and vigorously than *R. falconeri*. The flowers are cream, centre-blotched with deep crimson.

Another of my large-leaved choices is *R. fictolacteum*, a delightful species from western China. Its long narrow leaves are brown-felted on their undersides, and the tightly packed creamy-white flower trusses complete the perfect decorative picture. Most striking of them all, however, is another Chinese species, *R. sinogrande*. A well-known catalogue asserts that the leaves of this species sometimes grow more than $2\frac{1}{2}$ feet long and I can well believe that this is so, as some of those on my young specimen are already touching the two-foot mark. They are a polished dark green backed with a grey indumentum or coating. The loose flower trusses are creamy-white in colour and are splashed at their base with crimson. It is a species for gardens in mild areas.

Rhododendron macabeanum, another of the *grande* Series, makes an outstanding display, given suitable conditions. In colder districts, it will require light woodland shelter but the sight of its pale yellow, purple-spotted flowers in March is ample reward for this extra care and attention.

One of the loveliest of the pink-flowered species is *R. fargesii*, while *R. fortunei* is one of the most attractive members of the same group, with tremendous vigour and flowers of lilac-pink. It has transmitted its good qualities to its numerous offspring, including *R.* 'Luscombei' (*fortunei* × *thompsonii*), a glorious hybrid with large pink dark-throated blossoms; 'China' (*fortunei* × *wightii*), a strong-growing pale creamy-yellow; and Naomi (Aurora × *fortunei*), whose flowers are a soft lilac-pink suffused with buff.

Rhododendron fargesii itself is equally vigorous and free-flowering with flower trusses loosely packed with campanulate blossoms that are a deep pink in bud but open to a clearer pastel shade. One of the best late-flowering species is *R. discolor*, a 20-footer with long narrow leaves and gigantic pink flower trusses that open in June and July.

The dwarf rhododendron species have been dealt with in

T–E

a previous chapter (pp 69–71), but there are several other species of moderate growth that would enable the gardener whose space is restricted to plant an interesting collection. These include *R. campylocarpum*, *R. cinnabarinum* and its varieties, *R. orbiculare* and *R. thomsonii*.

Chapter Eight

Bringing the Garden Indoors

Twenty or thirty years ago, a chapter like this would probably have been titled 'Flowers for Cutting', a subject that, in those days, might easily have been disposed of in a thousand or so words. In such a chapter great importance would have been attached to flowers like roses, sweet peas, chrysanthemums and, of course, *Gypsophila paniculata*, the ubiquitous 'gyp', which would undoubtedly have received honourable mention as a filler-in for the house vases. Foliage plants for cutting might well have been restricted to a few tried-and-true favourites like maidenhair and asparagus fern, or, for grander table arrangements, the delicate long festoons of ivy or smilax.

Modern trends. Today, however, the whole subject of flowers for cutting has undergone a revolutionary change. The first faint rumblings of this were already audible in the Thirties, when the late Constance Spry started to do interesting things with cabbage leaves and cow parsley, while, since the war, the Mesdames Clements, Stevenson, Macqueen and a host of other talented ladies have brought to a peak of perfection the work that she initiated.

It is from such modest beginnings that the present National Association of Flower Arrangement Societies has emerged. It comprises approximately 700 affiliated societies whose membership totals more than 60,000.

Flower Arrangement. 'Doing the flowers' has become an aesthetic pursuit known as Flower Arrangement, a pursuit which can also become a competitive artistic exercise with a set of rules as complicated as the Marquess of Queensberry's and one in which few holds are barred.

But the trend goes even deeper than this and I sometimes suspect that the rapid growth of this (dare I quote ?) 'monstrous regiment of women' is all part of an underground movement expressly designed to give the so-called gentler sex a more important stake in the management of one of man's last strongholds, his garden. No longer is the lady of the garden content to pay it flying visits in order to snip off our choicest roses, dahlias and chrysanthemums for her flower vases, or containers, as we must now learn to call them.

An addiction to flower-arranging gives her, in addition, a heaven-sent opportunity to dictate what shall be grown and we soon find ourselves planting anything from blood-red spinach to exotic green lilies that cost more than most of us should afford.

Fortunately, there is a brighter side to this gloomy picture. Her interest in the down-to-earth fundamentals of gardening is frequently stimulated at the same time. This can be instrumental in encouraging more active participation, so that the gardener with a flower-arranging wife may often find that he has gained a useful working partner.

In all seriousness, however, it must be admitted that the cultivation of plants suitable for the flower arrangers has done much to widen the scope and broaden the outlook of many gardeners, introducing them to a new and interesting range of plants and affording them a greater appreciation of the sculptural and textural qualities of the plants they grow already.

Foliage for Cutting

One of the most important requirements of the flower arrangers is a plentiful supply of decorative foliage plants, since leaves form the basis and background of the vast majority of arrangements, acting as contrast and/or harmony to the flowers themselves. But not any foliage will do; the materials used must have at least some of the qualities of form and texture already mentioned.

Sword-like foliage is always in great demand for the backbone of the ultra-simplified arrangements currently in vogue.

This is provided by the leaves of numerous iris species, by ornamental grasses and some bamboos, by the grooved blades of *Curtonus paniculatus* (syn. *Antholyza paniculata*) which looks like a king-sized montbretia, and the more strap-shaped foliage of day lilies, agapanthus, crinums, nerines and the immense and stately New Zealand flax, *Phormium tenax*.

Plantain lilies. Equally popular are the plantain lilies or hostas, whose common name provides an apposite description of the shape of their leaves. Some are self-coloured, in other species and hybrids they are margined or splashed with a contrasting colour. In size they range from the gigantic blue-grey leaves of *H. sieboldiana* (*H. glauca*) which are 9 inches across and half as long again, to the diminutive *H. tardiflora*, whose foliage is quite narrow, glossy and a rich dark green in colour.

Good intermediate forms include the small *H. albomarginata*, which has broad, ivory-edged leaves; the large 'Thomas Hogg', with similar leaves; *H. crispula*, with wavy-edged leaves and wider white margins; *H. fortunei* 'Albo-picta', whose big leaves are soft yellow with a green edge as they unfurl and gradually turn all-green; and finally, *H. lancifolia*, whose leaves, as one might suppose from its name, are narrow and lance-shaped.

Hostas, which are still quite often referred to under their former name of Funkia, have a distinct preference for moist soil conditions. However, they are equally happy in sunlight or shadow, although when they are grown in the shade, their foliage will be more luxuriant, while in sunnier situations they will produce their graceful flower spikes in greater abundance. Plants growing in sunny positions will require regular and liberal watering during dry summer spells.

They are perhaps seen at their best out-of-doors in a waterside setting and, once planted, will need little attention. An annual application of well-rotted farmyard manure or compost will keep them healthy and flourishing. This can be applied either as a summer mulch or can be spread over the dormant – and incidentally, invisible – crowns in winter. This habit of hostas of disappearing completely from sight during the winter months means that winter tidying and forking over must be carried out with care, if damage to the plants is to be avoided.

Arums. Somewhat similar in shape to those of the hostas, but of an entirely different texture, are the decorative leaves of two arums, *Arum italicum marmoratum* and *A. pictum* (syn. *A. corsicum*), both of which are European relations of our native cuckoo-pint, *A. maculatum*, itself a useful source of foliage for spring arrangements. The leaves of the Italian variety are dark green with lighter veins and attractive mottling, while those of the Corsican species are even more striking, being marbled with grey, white and varying shades of green.

These arums have no particular soil preferences and are easily grown in sun or shade. Like the hostas, they will produce their typical greenish spathes more abundantly when growing in sunny situations.

Bergenia. The rounded, leathery leaves of the bergenias (formerly known as megaseas or giant saxifrages), are noteworthy for their long-keeping qualities in the house, lasting for a month or more in water. They are handsome in appearance at all times, but more particularly so in winter, when the leaves of some species turn a brilliant scarlet and others assume bronzy hues.

The leaves of *Bergenia cordifolia*, one of the species most widely grown, are an exception and retain their clear green colouring throughout the year. Those who prefer brighter leaf colour should grow the variety *purpurea*, whose leaves take on a distinctive purplish tinge in winter.

The named Ballawley Hybrid is probably the most outstanding member of this genus. This is a relatively new introduction from Ireland, with leaves 9 inches across that turn a vivid red in winter. Evening Glow is another attractive named form; its foliage is heart-shaped and a reddish-bronze in colour.

All the bergenias grow between 9 and 18 inches tall and the distinctive geometrical curves of their foliage make it ideal for contrasting with the vertical lines of iris and similar foliage. They will flourish in almost any soil and situation and those with limited garden space can safely plant them in tubs or other similar garden containers.

Intricate foliage. For arrangements with a more flowing line, foliage of more intricate design will be required. The ferny foliage of plants like bleeding heart (*Dicentra spectabilis*), shrubby rue, *Ruta graveolens*, and meadow rue, *Thalictrum glaucum*, will all prove useful in this connection. The leaves of *T. minus adiantifolium* are useful in smaller arrangements, their lacy construction being strongly reminiscent of the maiden-hair fern.

Acanthus. The acanthus, already mentioned for their liking for hot dry soil conditions, both the Italian *A. mollis latifolius* and the Southern European species, *A. spinosus*, are outstanding examples of plants whose foliage is of supreme sculptural beauty both in and out of doors. Both will need a certain amount of winter protection in colder districts until they are fully established.

Incidentally, many such partially tender plants can be grown in the open garden if they are afforded protection during the first few winters. All that is required is a shelter of sacking or polythene, supported on a light framework of canes, or a covering of bracken retained in position by fruit netting. This provides shelter from cold winds, which often do more harm than the severest frosts.

Plants which may require this form of protection include the Strawberry Tree, *Arbutus unedo*, ceanothus, the papery flowered Cistuses, tree heaths, escallonias, eucryphias, *Laurus nobilis* (the Sweet Bay), *Phormium tenax* (the New Zealand flax, mentioned earlier in the chapter) and the Japanese varieties of azalea.

Peonies. Peonies have long been esteemed for the beauty and keeping qualities of their perfect globular blooms, but the leaves of most species and varieties are equally valuable in arrangements. Particularly attractive, where the latter use is concerned, are the blue-grey, finely cut leaves of the yellow-flowered *P. mlokosewitschii*, mentioned in an earlier chapter (p 84), and those of the Moutan or tree peony, *P. suffruticosa*.

Foliage shrubs. The provision of foliage for cutting is not confined to herbaceous plants. Shrubs make their invaluable contributions in even more generous terms. The foliage of many has an attractive gloss, and camellias, mahonias, arbutus, *Choisya ternata* and many rhododendrons display this characteristic to a marked degree. Others, perhaps a little less highly polished, including *Elaeagnus* and *Magnolia grandiflora*, make a similar valuable contribution.

More distinctive in form are the finely-divided pinnate leaves of the Angelica Tree, *Aralia elata*, or those of the very similar *Sorbaria arborea glabrata*.

My wife particularly likes the glossy five-lobed leaves of the evergreen *Fatsia japonica*, a close relation of the aralias, for her arrangements. More than a foot across in mature specimens, the leaves are like those of a giant ivy, and there is a young plant growing away vigorously on the north wall of the cottage. In November, *F. japonica* produces clusters of ivory-white flowers that are followed by attractive black fruits.

Foliage trees. There are two trees, moderate enough in size for the average garden, which produce some of the most striking autumn leaf tints. *Cercidiphyllum japonicum* forms a small, round-headed tree with exceptionally finely coloured foliage. *Parrotia persica* is a good deal larger, but is relatively slow-growing. Its hazel-like leaves are a heart-warming sight when they assume their scarlet and gold autumn livery.

Where space permits, the Red Oak, *Quercus borealis maxima*, sometimes called *Q. rubra*, is indispensable. Its leaves, a good deal larger than those of the common oak, turn a more fiery scarlet than those of any other tree hardy in the British Isles with the possible exception of the Sweet Gum, *Liquidambar styraciflua*. They last well indoors and can be preserved for winter use by the method adopted for beech leaves. Sprays are cut just as they begin to colour and are placed in a deep vase or other similar container containing a mixture of half glycerine and half water. The ends of the twigs should be bruised or split; they are left to soak in this mixture until it is apparent from the appearance and feel of them that the glycerine has been absorbed.

Foliage roses. Several of the shrub roses are grown almost exclusively for the beauty of their foliage. The greyish-crimson 'bloomy' leaves of *Rosa rubrifolia* are a good example of these.

Other grey-leaved shrub roses, all in great demand for arrangements in which red predominates, are *R. fedtschenkoana*, *R. murielae* and Céleste.

Flowers for Cutting

Shrub roses. Where flowers are concerned not all tried-and-true favourites are acceptable to the arrangers. They dislike, for example, a surfeit of daisy-type flowers and, as far as roses are concerned, would much rather have old-fashioned cabbage roses and off-beat colours like purple and slate-grey.

In this I agree with them. My own preference is for the loose, natural beauty and rich fragrance of many of the older shrub and species roses, rather than for the frigid perfection of many of the newer hybrid teas, which I cover in Chapter Nine.

Nearly all the old roses arrange superbly and none better than the late Constance Spry's favourite Bourbons: Madame Pierre Oger, with its profusion of delicate shell-pink, perfectly globular blooms, the flamboyant carmine Mme Isaac Pereire and the bizarrely splashed Commandant Beaurepaire. These old roses have their modern counterparts in newer shrub roses, such as that named after Constance Spry herself, a deliciously fragrant clear pink centifolia-type rose, and the modern Rosemary Rose, both of which have been bred specially with the unspoilt charm of the old-fashioned roses in mind.

Others which find particular favour with me are the lavender-grey roses of which Prelude, Sterling Silver and Lilac Time are all good examples. Also enjoying a burst of popularity are the dainty Garnette roses, with miniature rosette-shaped blooms that last better than those of any other rose when cut. We can now obtain these delightful dwarfs in other colours besides the original red.

Green flowers. Two years ago, I was persuaded by 'you-know-who' to plant three specimens of the 'green' China rose, *R. chinensis viridiflora*. The catalogue description sounded revolting, but I have to admit, now that I have seen it in flower, that the small green buds, whose petals are streaked with reddish-brown, are extremely attractive in a strange kind of way and undoubtedly 'do' something for all-green arrangements.

At the time of writing this, green flowers are the arrangers' particular delight. Green is the 'in' colour, although I understand that there is a distinct trend towards a return to the bright primary colours so much in favour with our Victorian forebears. I satisfy the demand for green by growing plants such as bells of Ireland, *Molucella laevis*, various spurges, green-flowered tobacco plants, green Love-lies-bleeding (*Amaranthus caudatus* 'Viridis') and *Alchemilla mollis* whose greenish-yellow flowers are as useful as its foliage is attractive.

Other interesting green blooms are provided by the Green Woodpecker gladiolus with its tall, lime-green spikes, *Cobaea scandens*, a half-hardy but very vigorous climber with greenish-purple bells, and the Green Dragon and Green Magic strains of lily, whose out-of-this-world beauty justifies their cost.

Peonies. Peonies, of course, have been considered as top-ranking flowers for cutting since time immemorial. They rate very highly, too, where scent, colour, form and long-lasting qualities are concerned. They are, however, such a decorative asset in the pleasure garden that it is worth while, space permitting, to grow a separate batch of plants, possibly in the kitchen garden, specially for cutting.

Dahlias and Chrysanthemums. Dahlias also make useful cut flowers and once they begin to bloom we can cut-and-come again until the first heavy frost takes its toll. Both the outdoor and greenhouse chrysanthemums are valuable and long-lasting as cut flowers. They are an almost essential ingredient of autumn arrangements, and are even more important in providing warm colours into the New Year.

Flowering shrubs. Of the various shrubs that provide flowers for cutting, it is, generally speaking, those with the slowest rate of growth whose flowers are most eagerly sought after. Camellias, rhododendrons, azaleas and magnolias are all highly esteemed. My advice, therefore, to the owner of the new garden, who would like to be able to gather his blossoms in quantity, is to get them in right at the start as a part of the initial planting. It must, however, be remembered that all of these, with the exception of some magnolias, are lime-haters.

Excellent winter material is provided by shrubs such as *Viburnum fragrans*, *Chimonanthus praecox* and *Hamamelis*, with fragrance thrown in for good measure. *Viburnum tinus* (Laurustinus) gives masses of winter flowers allied to attractive evergreen foliage. The long grey-green tassels of *Garrya elliptica* catkins offer a welcome change from those of the hazel and pussy-willow.

From March onwards, shrubs provide a wealth of cutting material. *Forsythia*, flowering currant, *Spiraea*, broom and lilac are just a few that make their valuable spring and early summer contribution.

Hydrangeas. From mid-July onwards, hydrangeas, with their outstanding decorative and long-lasting qualities, will take the centre of the stage. Some people consider the giant flower-heads of the varieties of *Hydrangea macrophylla* to be somewhat too artificial for arrangements of live material, and prefer the conical, off-white flower trusses of *H. paniculata* 'Grandiflora'. The former type, however, are second to none for winter use in dried arrangements; there are few, if any, flowers that retain so well their original colour and beauty of form after being subjected to a drying process. The method used for hydrangeas differs from the one already described for leaves; the flowers are picked as soon as they are fully developed and are placed in a container of water, which should reach at least halfway up their stems. They are left in this until the water evaporates, after which they can be tied in bunches and hung up, head downwards, in a dry, airy place until required for use.

The list of shrub material available could continue almost indefinitely, if space permitted, and could include many exotics that require the protection of a cool greenhouse. But the material itself is only half the story. It is the skill, taste and ingenuity with which it is used that really counts.

Dried and Everlasting Flowers

It is not only living material that plays its part in flower arrangements, as already mentioned when hydrangeas were under discussion. In winter, dried arrangements evoke pleasant and nostalgic memories of sunnier, warmer days and at the same time fulfil a decorative function that is almost equal to that of their living counterparts.

Everlasting flowers are, of course, eminently suitable for this purpose, but these, today, can be supplemented by numerous other dried flowers, leaves, seedheads and twigs, all of which provide outstanding material for such winter arrangements.

Among the more useful of the everlastings proper – I prefer the French description *immortelles* – I would give high marks to the following: *Limonium latifolium* (*Statice latifolia*) a firmly established favourite of many years' standing, with clouds of minute blue flowers borne on wire-thin stems; *Anaphalis triplinervis*, a grey-leaved perennial that bears clusters of papery white flowers with yellow centres; the annual *Helipterum roseum* (*Acroclinium*) and *H. manglesii* (*Rhodanthe*), and *Limonium sinuatum* (*Statice sinuata*).

Eryngiums. Most of the members of the eryngium family are first-rate for drying. The best known of these is *Eryngium maritimum*, our native sea holly, whose spiny glaucous calyces are extremely attractive. Also attractive is *E. amethystinum*, with metallic-looking steel-blue stems and bracts, and Violetta, in which they are an intense violet-blue.

There is also a biennial species, sometimes irreverently known as Miss Willmott's Ghost, on account of the glaucous white collars surrounding the blue flowers that glisten almost phosphorescently on moonlight nights. Plants of this attractive species, *E. giganteum*, will seed themselves freely to provide fresh supplies annually if the surrounding soil is left relatively undisturbed.

The distinctive blue thistle-like flower heads of *E. tripartitum* spring from a rosette of leaves at ground level. Like all the others mentioned it colours more intensely when grown in full sunlight.

Others which dry well. Although not actually everlastings or semi-everlastings, others which dry well and retain much of their colour, include herbaceous peonies, delphiniums, and the plate-like flower heads of *Achillea filipendulina* (*A. eupatorium*).

The flowers should be picked as soon as they are fully open, tied loosely in bunches, and hung up in a cool and airy place to dry. Damp, muggy sheds or cellars and bunching too tightly are two of the commonest causes of loss from mildew.

Seedheads

It is not only dried flowers that are so highly esteemed; the seedheads of many plants can also add their decorative quota to the beauty of winter arrangements.

Lunaria rediviva is a perennial relation of the better-known biennial form of honesty. It has the advantage of not seeding itself like a weed and producing seedlings in every odd corner of the garden, as the biennial species is apt to do. The lilac-white flowers are followed by elliptical papery seed-containing discs, very similar to those of the latter.

Morina longifolia is a more uncommon perennial, well worth a place in the border as well as being valuable as a source of decorative seedheads. Its thistle-like rich green basal foliage throws up tall stout stems that bear whorls of hooded flowers that are followed by distinctive brown seedpods. The stems and seed containers dry well to provide an interesting and unusual constituent of larger winter bunches. This plant, which hails from Nepal, is one of many 'musts' for arrangers. It does best in moist, well-drained soils.

Heracleum mantegazzianum, a member of the *Umbelliferae* – the family to which cow-parsley, hemlock and carrots belong – which is a gigantic version of the cow parsley, often grows more than 6 feet tall. The wheel-like seedheads are magnificent in really large arrangements, with a majestic dignity all their own. My wife uses them in association with poppy heads and dried ears of sweet corn.

Irises. Good use can be made, as well, of the cinnamon-brown seedheads of *Iris* species. Those of *I. sibirica* are most commonly seen, but there are several lesser-known species which provide even more attractive specimens. These are *I. foetidissima* whose seedpods burst, as they ripen, to display rows of orange seeds, *I. ochraurea* and *I. ochroleuca,* in both of which yellow flowers are followed by handsome seedheads, and *I. pseudacorus variegata*, an unusual form of the common yellow flag iris, which combines the beauty of striped foliage with good heads for drying.

Other seedheads. Those who have room for arrangements on the grandest scale should not fail to grow the New Zealand Flax, *Phormium tenax*. Its seedheads are borne on 6-foot stems and are as useful as the leaves for really large pedestal arrangements. Among other out-of-the-ordinary kinds, there are those of the Crown Imperials, *Fritillaria imperialis*, like delicately wrought Chinese boxes, and the brown pods of that hard-to-get peony, *P. mlokosewitschii* which, like those of *Iris foetidissima*, split open to reveal tightly packed rows of lacquer red seeds.

Berries

Many shrubs make their most valuable contribution to the house vases in autumn and early winter, when they declare their annual dividend of brilliant berries and fruits.

Barberries and cotoneasters. In this, as in so many other garden contexts, barberries and cotoneasters are very much to the fore, providing a lavish display of berried twigs and branches that cut and last well indoors. We manage to make use of most of the varieties that we grow for this purpose, including *Berberis thunbergii*, *B. wilsonae* and *B. yunnanensis*, all of which add the quality of brilliant autumn foliage to the bright scarlet and coral of their fruits. *Cotoneaster frigidus*, *C. lacteus* and *C. microphyllus*, all carry heavy crops of red berries well into the winter, provided that the thrushes and blackbirds can be persuaded to leave them alone.

Other berries. Among my own favourite berrying shrubs are *Clerodendron trichotomum*, with turquoise fruits set, like jewels, in a ring of deep red bracts, and *Hypericum elatum*, a member of the St John's Wort family, with scarlet pea-sized fruits that turn black as they ripen. I wonder that this easy-to-grow shrub is not more commonly seen, so pleasing is the effect of the clusters of berries, in every stage from light red to black, set off by five tobacco-brown bracts and a pair of oval leaves. The variety to have is 'Elstead'.

Seedlings spring up everywhere in our cottage garden, and I am hoping to do something to boost its popularity by giving them away to gardening friends.

Grey Foliage

A chapter of this kind would hardly be complete without some mention of silver and 'evergrey' foliage which serves such a useful purpose in softening the impact of the more garish flower colours, and also provides an eminently suitable foil for those of paler and pastel shades.

Artemisias. Once again, shrubs are generous in their provision of material and the artemisias, in particular, probably include the largest number of silver-leaved species in any one genus. Undoubtedly, the best known of these is *Artemisia abrotanum*, known affectionately by countless gardeners and non-gardeners as Old Man. Its other popular names are Lad's Love and Southernwood and the feathery grey-green foliage, so spicily fragrant when crushed, has made it a firm favourite with generations of cottagers.

But the lesser-known species are more beautiful than this. *A. arborescens* and *A. canescens* both have foliage as intricately cut as fine lace. The former, however, is slightly tender and needs winter protection in most districts. In contrast to the 2 to 3 feet of the other species, *A. canescens* grows only 18 inches high so that massed groups of this species make an unusually attractive ground cover that looks particularly fine in association with taller evergreen shrubs or as carpeting under the old-fashioned shrub roses.

Lambrook Silver, a named variety of *A. absinthium* – would this be the plant that gives *absinthe* its distinctive aniseed flavour ? – is another extremely decorative form, with coarsely cut foliage of sterling silver. All those already mentioned are European species. The North American species, *A. ludoviciana*, has willow-like leaves of silvery-white, but its named form, Silver Queen, which is identical in colour, has the typical cut foliage of its European relations. *A. gnaphalodes* has willow-like leaves which are dusted with silver like those of a 'dusty miller' auricula. All the species and varieties mentioned in this paragraph are herbaceous perennials.

All these artemisias, and, indeed, most silver or grey-leaved plants, display their characteristic colouring to better effect when they are grown in full sunlight. Apart from that single requirement, they are undemanding and will thrive in any ordinary well-drained soil. Lad's Love is even more accommodating and, provided it is given a place in the sun, will flourish in the poorest of soils. This probably accounts for its universal popularity as a garden plant for so many years.

Senecios and olearias. Both the senecios and the olearias are sun-lovers and many species of each are noteworthy for their silvered foliage. It must be borne in mind that most silver and grey-leaved shrubs seldom winter well in industrial and urban areas and are commonly seen at their best in seaside districts. *Olearia haastii*, however, is an exception to this in being tolerant of town conditions. It is the best-known species of the latter group, while *Senecio greyii*, of which we see *rather* too much in seaside municipal gardens, is representative of the former. *S. laxifolius* is almost identical in appearance to the latter, and easier to grow inland.

Those who practise garden one-upmanship and like to grow something 'different' should try *S. leuchostachys*, a delightfully slender silvery-white wall shrub, which likes a south or west aspect. There is a fine specimen of this shrub to be seen on the wall of the laboratory at Wisley.

In a new garden, for the first few years, the would-be Julia Clements will have to be content with annuals and perennials to provide that much sought-after white and silver foliage. Three plants that immediately come to mind are the giant grey-white Scots thistle, *Onopordon acanthium*, which one nurseryman describes in his catalogue in lyric terms that I could not hope to emulate – 'imagine a leafy, prickly grey-white thistle, stems all ribbed and flanged with grey flounces and making a branching candelabra of grey thistle-heads'. The other two are the biennial, formerly known as *Verbascum*

Broussa and now saddled with the far less attractive name of *V. bombyciferum*, and the ever-popular Lambs' Ears, *Stachys lanata*.

Once planted, the verbascum will keep you company for ever since it seeds itself, not freely enough to become a nuisance, but a season never goes by without the appearance of half a dozen seedlings in unexpected corners of the garden.

Anaphalis triplinervis, a grey-leaved perennial already mentioned for its 'everlasting' flowers, is also useful for its foliage.

Twisted Branches

In conclusion I ought to mention three shrubs which are valuable to those who specialize in Japanese-style arrangements if they have room enough in the garden. They are grown purely for the curious effect of their tortuous and twisted branches. These are *Salix matsudana* 'Tortuosa', an off-beat member of the willow family, *Corokia cotoneaster*, whose wire-thin twigs produce a tracery reminiscent of a filigree work, and *Corylus avellana* 'Contorta', whose spirally-twisted branches have earned it the name 'corkscrew hazel'.

Chapter Nine

Modern Roses in Small Gardens

In a previous book, *Planning and Planting the Small Garden*, I devoted very little space to roses – in actual fact, only a few pages – and a number of readers have taken me to task for this summary treatment of the Queen of Flowers.

The terrible truth of the matter is that, until three or four years ago, I could raise only the most limited enthusiasm for the rose as a garden flower although I have always considered it second to none for cutting. But the revival of interest in the old roses and their use, together with floribundas in the shrub border, made me do a good deal of re-thinking on this particular subject.

By the time that I had become completely enslaved to shrub roses, I found that my interest has spread to the cultivation of roses in general.

In this I was helped, I suppose, to no small extent, by the fact that the cottage into which I recently moved could only be described as the proverbial 'bower of roses'. The previous owner, a well-known and much-loved stage and television actress, had gone in for them in a big way. Countless arches and pergolas were festooned with ramblers and climbers of every variety, colour and description. The west wall of the house supported a venerable and vigorous New Dawn (or it might have been truer to say that the rose supported the west wall!), while the south front had a vigorous Climbing Mme Caroline Testout and a lovely large terracotta climber whose name I have yet to discover.

There were few bush roses, apart from a number of attractive rugosas, a hedge of the Great or Small Maiden's Blush, and some rose species, but the beds and borders were dotted haphazardly with a selection of standards.

In our first summer at the cottage, every day was a field day for the flower arranger of the family. For the first time ever, she could gather roses by the armful without giving a thought to the effect on the garden display. Soon arrangements featuring the Queen of Flowers burgeoned in every room and in every possible container and context.

Roses can be used with equal effect in either a formal or an informal setting or in gardens large or small. Hybrid teas and hybrid perpetuals lend themselves to the former treatment, preferably in beds of rectangular or other regular shapes, separated by paths of brick, paving or well-kept grass.

I have already discussed roses as hedging plants in Chapter Four. Mention has also been made of old-fashioned roses and miniature kinds. The present chapter, therefore, deals only with the more orthodox rose groups, such as hybrid teas, floribundas, climbing and rambler roses.

Floribunda Roses

The tremendous growth in popularity of floribunda roses since the war and the host of new recruits to their ranks have greatly widened the scope of the rose as a garden plant. Although most of these are first-rate for bedding, they look just as well in association with shrubs and the perceptive garden planner will make good use of them in this manner, massing them in groups and bays at the front of the shrub border.

Hybrid polyanthas. Floribunda roses are the result of crossing polyantha roses, which were dwarf plants that bore their flowers in large clusters, with the hybrid teas or musk roses. The first crosses were single or semi-double and the resulting hybrid polyanthas, known as Poulsen roses from the name of their originator Svend Poulsen, enjoyed a tremendous vogue in the Twenties and Thirties.

Many older gardeners will remember these roses with

affection. The pink Else Poulsen was one of the first on the scene, while others like Karen and Kirsten Poulsen bore the names of other members of the family.

Origin of floribundas. It was these hybrid polyanthas, crossed with the musks and hybrid teas, that produced the multitudes of exciting floribunda roses that are such a common feature of present-day gardens. In the main, they are a good deal more vigorous than the hybrid teas and perpetuals, with a long flowering season and great resistance to disease. As a means of providing colour during the summer and early autumn they are probably unsurpassed by any other shrub.

A host of new varieties appears each year in the rose growers' catalogues with such monotonous regularity that the newcomer to gardening might well be excused if he finds his initial choice difficult to make. It is possible, however, that the new plant patenting laws, giving growers the sole rights over their new introductions for a number of years, may be instrumental in stemming this flood of innovations.

Selecting floribundas. For those who find the task of selection difficult, there is a hard core of popular varieties that have proved themselves, many of which seem likely to remain high in garden popularity for some years to come.

Among the best of the present-day varieties are such well-loved floribundas as Iceberg, Evelyn Fison, Elizabeth of Glamis, Pink Parfait and Orange Sensation. Queen Elizabeth, first introduced as long ago as 1955, is still a firm favourite. This was one of the first of the floribundas to have individual blooms of the HT type. These, of a lovely clear pink, are borne both singly and in trusses.

Where bedding requirements are concerned, however, Queen Elizabeth has a disadvantage. This is its uncontrollable vigour. My own plants, in spite of regular and fairly drastic pruning, reached a height of 10 feet in their third season and have repeated this beanstalk performance every year since. Queen Elizabeth, however, is a rose that no one should be without in the garden although I feel it is more suitable for the shrub border than for formal bedding purposes.

Masquerade, in spite of newer introductions with similar

colour-change characteristics, still retains its popularity. The buds start out a deep yellow, changing to pink as they open and gradually deepening to a dark red. The large flower trusses contain blooms at every stage of this development. These provide a harlequin pattern of brilliant colour.

So far, pure yellows have been relatively scarce among the ranks of floribundas. There is, however, one outstanding example in Allgold, a brilliant golden-yellow rose that is far and away the finest in this particular colour range. Others well worth growing are Gold Gleam, with its larger flowers, Arthur Bell (but this has a tendency to fade), Golden Treasure and a new dwarf floribunda, Kim.

A floribunda of recent introduction that has made considerable impact is the highly original News, in which the old gallica rose Tuscany has been mated with Lilac Charm to produce a flower which is of a burgundy hue; an entirely new break which is satisfying to the lovers of both the old and the new.

Hybrid Teas

For use in formal bedding schemes, I still prefer the hybrid teas, although in our parks and public gardens the floribundas seem to be taking over as far as this form of rose growing is concerned. There is, however, nothing to compare with the perfection of the shapely blooms of well-grown hybrid teas. You would, for instance, have to go a long way to find any other type of rose with the sculptured beauty of the aptly named Perfecta.

I planted six bushes when this rose was first introduced in 1957. The blooms are a medium pink, gradually lightening in tone to a pinkish-yellow at the base of the petals. Much as I like the old-fashioned shrub roses, Perfecta, for me, at any rate, personifies all that is most typical of the rose, including that most important quality, fragrance.

Selecting hybrid teas. The choice of suitable varieties of hybrid tea for the garden of average size is no less difficult than the selection of floribundas, since new introductions have been appearing since the war in equally large numbers.

Collections. Growers' collections give good value for money, but to enjoy the beauty of individual varieties to the full, at least three specimens should be planted, not only for garden effect, but also in order that enough blooms of one kind are available for cutting. In fact, even in a fairly small garden, six of a kind would not be excessive, if roses are to be one of the main preoccupations of its owner.

I prefer, therefore, to make my own choice and, if possible, to see them growing and flowering under nursery conditions. The glass-grown rose that causes gasps of admiration at Chelsea may not always stand up so well to inspection when it blooms, at its proper season, out-of-doors.

Catalogues. If this is not possible, however, catalogues today, with the growing verisimilitude of colour photography, are becoming increasingly reliable as a guide. Even though we must take some of the descriptions with a pinch of the proverbial salt, the photographs are often fairly authentic. Only personal experience, however, will show how the varieties illustrated will stand up to your particular conditions of soil and situation.

This, of course, is true of floribundas as well as hybrid teas, but the former, generally speaking, are so free-flowering and vigorous that we are more able to take them on trust from their catalogue descriptions.

I have grown satisfactorily practically all the varieties of hybrid tea that follow. They are mainly fairly new introductions that have won almost universal acclaim for their good all-round qualities.

Reds. These, more than any others, should have special qualities both of petal texture and fragrance. Somehow, we naturally expect a red rose to be strongly scented and velvety in texture.

Josephine Bruce possesses both these qualities in good measure, with petals like crimson velvet and a delicious and penetrating fragrance. Madame Louis Laperrière is another with similar characteristics which has usurped the place of the older favourite, Etoile de Hollande. Few catalogues now list the latter, although it is a scented rose well worth growing. If they do, they generally add the comment: superseded by Mme Louis Laperrière.

Both the last-mentioned rose and Josephine Bruce have Crimson Glory as their pollen parent. This, too, is a red rose worth growing for its large and shapely flowers with velvety crimson petals.

Mention red roses and most people will say 'Ena Harkness'. This is a particularly vigorous rose that does well even in poor soils. Some catalogues list it as scented, but the perfume could scarcely be described as overpowering. My first choices among the reds, therefore, would always be Josephine Bruce, Madame Louis Laperrière, Alec's Red and Ernest H. Morse.

Yellows. In spite of all that has been written about the fine qualities of Peace, it would not be my ideal choice where yellow hybrid teas are concerned, especially if I wanted it for bedding. Peace is an awkward bedfellow, and its tall and branching growth is really more suited, like that of Queen Elizabeth, to the shrub border rather than the formal bedding scheme. Hard pruning does not solve the problem, but only seems to act as a spur to Peace's ambition to outgrow and outcrowd its neighbours.

Nevertheless, it still deserves the tremendous reputation it has enjoyed since its introduction in 1945. Although lacking in fragrance, the outsize pale yellow flowers, flushed with pink at the margins of their petals, are magnificent, not least because of the admirable manner in which they are set off by the large, polished foliage.

Pink and Carmine. Some of the old favourites are still well represented in this colour range, including Ophelia and Madame Butterfly, Lady Sylvia and Picture. All of these are pale pink roses. Of the newer varieties, Pink Favourite, a deep pink, and My Choice, an intensely fragrant rose whose pink petals are backed with pale yellow, are both in the top class.

Picture, which flowers abundantly, with clear rose-pink blooms of medium size that blend beautifully with the deep green foliage, is among the most attractive of the pink roses suitable for bedding. It is highly weather-resistant and the only black mark against it is its lack of fragrance.

Those looking for a 'typical' pink rose could not find a better choice than Silver Lining, a 1958 introduction. This had the distinction of being selected by the National Rose Society for presentation to HM the Queen in commemoration of Prince Andrew's birth. It has been honoured, too, with the Royal Horticultural Society's Award of Merit. Its silvery-pink fragrant blossoms cannot fail to delight.

Bicolours. One of the best-known and earliest examples of a bi-coloured rose is Daily Mail, alias Mme Edouard Herriot, which was introduced early in the twenties. This is a type of rose that has become increasingly popular in recent years.

One of the finest of the present-day bicolours is Piccadilly, a scarlet rose with a yellow reverse. Isabel de Ortiz is another elegant variety of distinguished lineage. It has Peace as one parent, Perfecta as the other. Isabel de Ortiz has a silvery pink reverse to its cerise-pink blooms.

Gail Borden, whose deep rose-pink petals are backed with creamy yellow, is still well worth growing. The flowers are classic in shape – large, pointed and borne on long stems.

Among the newer roses, Chicago Peace is one of the more interesting. Its blooms are a blend of phlox-pink and canary-yellow.

Vermilion. No mention of hybrid teas would be complete without mention of Super Star and Fragrant Cloud, those two outstanding introductions of the Sixties. Although the luminous, light vermilion colouring of the former makes it rather difficult to place in the rose garden, its superb qualities, which include tremendous vigour, great resistance to disease, rich, fruity scent, freedom of flowering and brilliant colouring, make it a 'must' for all rose growers. Fragrant Cloud, a geranium-red rose, shares all these sterling qualities and both are, in addition, intensely fragrant.

White. White HT roses are always a rather doubtful quantity in the garden. They are among the first to succumb to 'balling' of the blooms and browning of the petals in bad weather.

There are few finer whites than that old favourite, Frau Karl Druschki, which first saw the light of day before World War One. Pascali is one of the best of the newer white roses for garden display as well as being excellent for cutting, with Virgo and Memoriam as doubtful runners-up.

Other Colours. Wendy Cussons, officially described as 'cerise flushed scarlet' – a description that hardly does justice to its glorious wine-red colouring – has a delightful fragrance and is one of the finest roses to emerge in the past two decades. Blue Moon, too, is an attractive 'blue' rose, silvery-lilac in colour, delicately scented and a delight to the flower arrangers.

Planting

Correct depth of planting is of the utmost importance where roses are concerned. Everyone knows, of course, that roses are not normally grown on their own roots but on a variety of wild or cultivated stocks that include our native dog rose, *Rosa canina*, and a number of briars. There are various reasons for this. The first and most important is that roses budded on to these rootstocks give a far higher proportion of 'takes' than they would from cuttings, and secondly, the resulting plants, in the majority of cases, are far more vigorous than those raised from cuttings.

Depth of planting. It is essential, therefore, when planting, to ensure that the original point of union between scion and rootstock is approximately at soil level.

I was recently introduced to a planting method that not only ensures that your roses are planted at the correct depth, but also makes the actual operation a simple one-man job. This is how you proceed.

Method. Having prepared the planting site, you take out holes to a depth and of a size sufficient to allow room for the roots to be spread out without bunching or over-crowding. A fairly light stake is then driven into the centre of the hole and another is laid across the surface of the soil at right-angles to the former. The rose to be planted is temporarily secured to the vertical stake with the point of union level with the horizontal one. A plastic tie twisted round main stem and upright stake makes an excellent temporary tie for this purpose.

Both hands are then available for filling in the planting hole.

Remember to tread the plant well during the filling-in process, unless the soil is too heavy and sticky when it is better to let Time and Nature do the job for you. The alternative is to use a mixture of equal parts of peat, leafmould or well-rotted compost, mixed with dry sifted soil and generously laced with bonemeal.

Climbers and Ramblers

One way of extending the scope of our rose-growing in the smaller garden is by the use of rambling and climbing roses. It is important, however, to be quite sure that we know exactly what is meant by the two terms 'climber' and 'rambler'.

Differences between climbers and ramblers. The latter, with only a few exceptions, provide only one flush of blossom; their display normally extends through the second half of June and part of July. While it lasts, this display can be outstandingly brilliant, but for the rest of the summer, we have to resign ourselves to a long, flowerless period relieved only by not particularly interesting foliage, which in the case of many ramblers is highly susceptible to mildew.

Climbing roses, however, share all the fine qualities of the hybrid teas and floribundas, including their continuity of flowering throughout the summer and autumn. Many of them, in fact, are climbing 'sports' of popular bedding varieties, so that, among others, we can grow a climbing Ena Harkness, Lady Sylvia, and Masquerade. These three are not continuous-flowering but there are others, including Handel, Pink Perpetue, Altissimo and Bantry Bay, which are.

Position. Climbers and ramblers can be grown on walls and fences, but in such positions they are more than ever susceptible to mildew and black spot. This can be avoided to a certain extent by training them on wires or trellises fixed 6 inches or so away from the wall surface so that a freer circulation of air is obtained.

The best and most effective way of growing them, however, is on posts, pillars, pergolas or trellises. A rose walk, bordered by brick or stone pillars, linked by wooden cross beams, planted with climbing roses, makes one of the most pleasing of garden features; a similar and less costly, but also less permanent, effect can be achieved by the use of stout timber uprights.

Ramblers. My choice of ramblers would be the old-fashioned Dorothy Perkins (soft pink) and Emily Gray (golden-yellow) – the former is particularly susceptible to mildew and should not, therefore, be planted on a wall – and American Pillar, another old favourite (deep carmine-pink with a white centre). Violette is an unusual rambler, deep violet in colour, that makes an effective contrast to the flesh pink of Dr W. Van Fleet or the yellow Easlea's Golden Rambler, while the rambler that has everything, scent, size, vigour, and brilliant colour – the phenomenal Albertine – is a 'must' in every rose garden.

Climbers. A rose walk of this kind should contain a judicious mixture of climbers and ramblers to ensure a continuous display throughout the summer months. Among the finest climbers that I have grown I rate the following very highly: Climbing Mrs Sam McGredy (copper-salmon), Climbing Shot Silk (a fragrant orange-cerise), Climbing Spek's Yellow (without doubt the finest yellow climber) and for those who like its ever-changing kaleidoscope of colour, Climbing Masquerade.

Finally, there are two outstanding climbers that should find a place in every garden. The first of these, Mermaid, an evergreen *bracteata* rose, with enormous sulphur-yellow single flowers, sometimes takes a season or two to get under way, but once started there is no holding it. So vigorous is it, that it will thrive and flower even on a north wall.

The other, New Dawn, is in fact a rambler, but it is a notable exception to the once-flowering rule, since it is smothered in large trusses of flesh-pink, delicately fragrant blooms, each a perfect rose in itself, from the time it starts to flower in June until very late autumn.

Pruning. The procedure varies with these two categories. The flowering shoots of the 'single-shot' ramblers can be cut right out at any time after the blossoms have faded; strong and vigorous new shoots develop each year from the base to carry the following year's crop of flowers.

Climbers, on the other hand, are pruned fairly lightly, to encourage the formation of healthy side shoots which are tied in as they develop. Only dead and worn out wood is removed completely – new shoots developing from the base or near it will serve as replacements.

With the climbing sports of the hybrid tea roses, care must be taken not to prune too drastically, especially when they are first planted, as too severe pruning can cause them to revert to bush habit.

Chapter Ten

Fragrance of Flower and Foliage

So far, we have talked a great deal about the decorative qualities of garden plants, their architectural and sculptural value, their beauty of form, flower and foliage, and other similar characteristics that go to make a successful garden display.

But there is one other vitally important characteristic – one, too, that almost defies description – and that is fragrance. Even if it were possible to describe it in adequate terms, we should still be unable to find two people who could agree on a definition of this elusive quality as applied to the majority of our scented garden plants.

We actually describe most flower perfumes by comparison. Such and such, we say, smells like vanilla; another has the scent of cloves, and when it comes to the subtle distinctions between the scents of different roses we run the whole gamut of perfumes, from tea to apples and are hard put to it to find sufficient standards of comparison.

But everyone will agree that a garden without fragrance would scarcely be worthy of the name. When we are planning, therefore, we should make certain that our planting plan contains a generous quota of plants that are noteworthy for their perfume.

Many shrubs, of course, are distinguished for the fragrance of their blossom, but it is, perhaps, during the winter months that shrubs make their greatest contribution where perfume is concerned. The blooms of the winter-flowering kinds would hardly be called showy, but many of them make up for this shortcoming by the sweetness and intensity of their perfume which, on still sunny winter days, will scent the air for yards around, while a sprig or two brought indoors is enough to fill a whole room with fragrance.

Winter

Fragrant viburnums. The first of these winter-flowering shrubs to come into flower is *Viburnum fragrans*, which begins to open its pink-tinted blossoms in late October or early November and continues to produce them successively until early spring. Those who plant it for the first time should not be disappointed if their plant remains flowerless for the first few years after planting. *V. fragrans* takes some time to settle down to blossom production and although it may flower sporadically a year or so after planting, it takes five or six years before it comes into full production. The hybrid *V. bodnantense* 'Dawn' has a richer pink flush and a graceful habit.

In addition to the pinkish form there is one with white flowers, *candidissimum*, and a more dwarf variety *compactum*, ideal for the smaller garden. Although the type grows from 12 to 15 feet tall, the latter, with a spread of similar dimensions, is less than half that height.

Witch-hazels. Flowering at a much earlier stage in their development – a bush only a year or so old will be covered in blossom – the witch-hazels never fail to wreathe their grey twigs with curious spidery primrose-scented blossoms early each January. *Hamamelis mollis*, the species most commonly seen, has narrow, strap-like yellow petals, but there is also a lovely variety, *pallida*, whose flowers are a paler, but more striking yellow.

Hamamelis mollis is a native of China, but *H. japonica*, which hails from Japan, was the first oriental species to arrive in this country, more than a hundred years after *H. virginiana* had been introduced from North America. The flowers of *H. japonica* have purple calyces. The named variety Carmine Red has flowers for which the description 'dull mahogany' is to my mind, more suitable. *H.* × *intermedia* 'Flavo purpurescens' is a variety which is seldom seen and whose flowers are suffused with wine-red.

All the witch-hazels prefer a permanently moist root run and will not do well if lime is present in the soil in any quantity. There is a fine specimen in my garden camouflaging the top of the septic tank. It flourishes greatly – no doubt on account of the slight seepage that keeps the surrounding soil well supplied with moisture.

Daphnes. The daphnes are a delightful family and the great majority of its members are endowed with intense fragrance, including our native mezereon, *Daphne mezereum*, and the evergreen *D. odora*, both of which come into bloom in February. *D. mezereum* is completely hardy and its purple, hyacinth-scented flower spikes will often start to open towards the end of January. There is a white form, *alba*, but neither this nor the purple form is particularly long-lived. Fresh stocks, however, can easily be raised from seed, provided you protect the poisonous berries from birds, who gobble them up voraciously without coming to any harm.

Daphne odora is slightly tender and deserves a position where it is sheltered from north and east. Both these early-flowering species are ideal plants for the smallest garden, *D. mezereum* being only $3\frac{1}{2}$ to 4 feet tall, while *D. odora* makes a low-growing bush about 4 feet in height with a spread of about 6 feet. The exquisitely scented flowers of this species are a soft purplish-red and are borne in clusters at the end of the stems. There is an uncommon variety, 'Aureo-marginata', whose leaves are edged with gold. It is said to be slightly hardier than the type.

The Winter Sweet. No winter-flowering shrub has a more penetrating fragrance than the Winter Sweet, *Chimonanthus praecox* (syn. *C. fragrans*) whose waxen yellow flowers, centre-blotched with purple, follow close on those of the witch-hazels. Although quite hardy, this shrub is seen at its best in a sheltered position and I would always find room for it on a south or west wall where the sunshine of warm early spring days will bring out to the full its elusive but intense fragrance.

There are several garden forms, including one with flowers of pure yellow, *luteus*, and another, *grandiflorus*, whose flowers are a good deal larger than those of the type. Neither of these, however, is as fragrant as the common form. Like the winter-flowering viburnum mentioned earlier, the Winter Sweet takes some time to reach the flowering stage.

Since the Winter Sweets are Chinese relations of the Carolina Allspice or *Calycanthus floridus* (see p 123) (they were formerly known as *Calycanthus fragrans*) it is not surprising to find that the wood is also aromatic and is used by oriental housewives, tied in bunches to scent their linen presses, in the same way that lavender is used in this country.

Spring

Siphonosmanthus and Osmanthus. March is rather short on scented shrubs. I can call to mind only one, *Siphonosmanthus delavayi* (formerly known as *Osmanthus delavayi*), that actually starts to flower during the month and this does not come into bloom until the month's end. This is another Chinese shrub, which, like many others of eastern origin, was cultivated for many hundreds of years in temple gardens before being introduced to western gardens.

This shrub is completely hardy, but in very cold districts it may need slight protection during its first winter in the garden. A small tent of sacking or polythene, supported by canes or stakes so that the protective material does not come into contact with the evergreen foliage, will be sufficient for this purpose.

The dark green, heart-shaped foliage makes a perfect background for the pure white tubular flowers, half an inch in length. These appear when the plants are quite young. *Siphonosmanthus delavayi* is useful either in the border or as a wall shrub. It will appreciate the shelter afforded by the latter situation, if it is planted on the south or west.

There is another species to be found in some catalogues, not to be confused with the spring-flowering one. This is *Osmanthus ilicifolius* with holly-like leaves and inconspicuous white fragrant flowers, which begin to open in autumn.

Viburnums. I always think of the viburnums as 'shrubs for all seasons', since there is scarcely any day in the year when one of the numerous species is not making its contribution to the beauty of the garden. After *Viburnum fragrans* (see p 116) has finished it will be the turn of the carnation-scented Korean species, *V. carlesii* and its related hybrids, *V. burkwoodii* (*carlesii* × *utile*) and *V. juddii* (*carlesii* × *bitchiuense*), to make their fragrant contribution. The hybrid *V. carlcephalum*, a cross between *V. carlesii* and *V. macrocephalum*, is a good deal more vigorous than the two just mentioned as it grows 8 feet tall with flowers that can be as much as 5 inches across. It flowers in May and makes a good follow-on for the earlier flowering forms, where space is sufficient to warrant its inclusion. The flowers of all these viburnums are tinged with pink at the bud stage but open to pure white or the faintest of pinks.

Corylopsis. *C. spicata* is not totally hardy but quite safe in the shelter of a patch of woodland where it will be protected from north and east winds. In fact, it has naturalized itself in the woods that adjoin the cottage, and we can always depend on the five or six plants that grow there for branches of the pale yellow pendent blossoms that smell so delicately of primroses and cowslips.

It is closely related to the witch hazel and in addition to the one just mentioned there are other attractive species including *C. glabrescens*, a tall-growing native of Japan, *C. pauciflora*, which does not exceed 4 feet in height, and the elegant twelve-footer, *C. willmottiae*, whose flowers are larger and more fragrant than those of *C. spicata*.

The faint greenish tinge to the flowers, contrasting with the dark brown of the bare stems, makes *C. willmottiae* a popular subject for spring flower arrangements. It looks particularly well with daffodils or narcissi.

Summer

Varied pleasures. From April until the end of June there is no shortage of scented shrubs in the well-planned garden. Lilacs drench the air with their fragrance – surely one of the most delicious flower scents – and there will be the peppery scent of brooms, with the unusual pineapple scent of the Moroccan species, *Cytisus battandieri*. Mock oranges (*Philadelphus*) will distil their penetrating perfume in June, and on the house walls, jasmine and honeysuckle will waft their fragrance through the house windows.

Roses. The true rose fragrance is, of course, second to none in the garden and high up in the list where this characteristic is concerned come the old, so-called 'shrub' roses, the musks, bourbons, gallicas and rugosas, all of which literally saturate the surrounding air with their never-cloying perfume.

The credit for the recent revival in popularity of these roses is due almost entirely to one man, Mr Graham S. Thomas who has opened up new avenues of trouble-free rose growing for countless gardeners since his first book, *The Old Shrub Roses*, appeared in the 1950s.

The great advantage of these old roses lies in the fact that they can be treated in almost exactly the same manner as hardy shrubs, which, of course, is what they are. Instead of the tedious operations of drastic annual pruning and subsequent disbudding, as well as complicated feeding and spraying routines that generations of rose growers have inflicted on us, shrub roses need only a minimum of attention; no more in fact than any other hardy and vigorous flowering shrub.

All we need to do is to allow them to go on 'doin' what comes naturally' with just an occasional going over with the secateurs to cut out dead wood and weak or straggling shoots. Grown in this way, they will increase in beauty from year to year, and, for the gardener with twenty or thirty yards of border to spare, there are few more attractive ways of filling it than by planting it with a collection of these old shrub roses in conjunction with low-growing shrubs, spring- and summer-flowering bulbs, lilies, and suitable ground cover plants.

Once you have seen them growing you will want to order dozens of different species and varieties, without giving a thought either to the cost or to the space available in the garden for planting them when they arrive.

Of the many I have grown from time to time, almost all have been strongly scented, for as far as I am concerned, a rose without scent is a contradiction in terms. This is not to deny,

however, that a good many modern HTs and a few floribundas
are indeed richly scented. Among the HTs are Super Star,
Fragrant Cloud, Alec's Red, Wendy Cussons, Ena Harkness,
Ernest H. Morse and plenty more; and among floribundas we
have, for example, Orange Sensation, Elizabeth of Glamis,
Dearest and Scented Air.

Honeysuckle. Honeysuckle and jasmine, as I mentioned
earlier, distil their heavy fragrance on the house walls in summer and one of the showiest examples of the former is the
hybrid *Lonicera americana*, a vigorous grower whose rose-
purple flowers, striking for a honeysuckle, are lined with a
delicate apricot.

Jasmine. *Jasminum officinale*, with its vigorous twining habits
and finely cut foliage, is the best form to grow for summer
fragrance. It shares with the lilies and tuberoses a somewhat
funereal scent, but for those who do not mind perfumes that
are on the cloying side, the summer jasmine is without rival. It
can be rather difficult to restrain, once it is established, and
needs quite a bit of attention where pruning and tying are concerned. At the cottage I have switched to *J. beesianum*, a species
that is far less rampant. The flowers, which are a deep rose in
colour, are just as fragrant as those of the commoner form, while
the shrub itself has a much less coarse and vigorous habit.

There is an attractive Chinese evergreen species whose fragrant white flowers are borne in clusters. This is well worth
growing if you can give it the shelter of a south wall. *J.
stephanense*, which is a cross between *J. beesianum* and *J.
officinale* and inherits the better qualities of both, has fragrant
blossoms of pale pink.

Clematis flammula. In July and August, at the same time
as the jasmines are in flower, *Clematis flammula* will be filling
the air with the penetrating scent from its masses of tiny stellate
blossoms, so thickly borne that they practically smother the
entire plant. My specimen was planted on the south wall of the
cottage last year and pruned back nearly to ground level this
February at the same time being generously dosed with compost and bonfire ash; it is already well past the junction of
walls and hanging tiles and half way to roof level. *Erica carnea*

King George is planted at its base to provide the shade its roots appreciate. It is flanked by a wisteria and a passion flower, through whose branches it can ramble as it pleases. I shall cut it back severely each spring and give it 'the mixture as before' as far as feeding is concerned.

While scented shrubs delight us in spring and summer, annuals, perennials and bulbous plants will have been contributing their share to the fragrance of the garden. Sweet-scented hyacinths, jonquils and narcissus mingle their scents with the unforgettable fragrance of wallflowers, while sweet rocket, sweet sultan, sweet peas – all of them aptly named – as well as other annuals and biennials will swell the tide of perfume.

Perfume at night. Certain plants are at their most fragrant after dusk has fallen and the masculine scent of the tobacco plant will join with those of the evening primrose and night-scented stock to fill the darkness with their heavy fragrance.

Fragrant Leaves

Aromatic shrubs. Fragrance of foliage, as well as of flowers, is a quality with which many plants are richly endowed. In general, shrubs with scented foliage tend to be low-growing and compact, so that we can find room for them at the edge of the border or at the side of paths, where we can pause to crush their scented leaves and savour their spicy aroma.

One of the best-known of these is *Artemisia abrotanum*, the grey-leaved Old Man mentioned earlier. Very similar in appearance, but with longer and more finely dissected foliage and a distinctive fragrance of lemon verbena, is one of the taller cotton lavenders, *Santolina neapolitana*. This is a shrub for warm, well-drained sunny positions. *Aloysia triphylla* (*Lippia citriodora*) has lemon-scented leaves. It likes the shelter of a warm wall.

Laurus nobilis, the Sweet Bay, is a comparative rarity among the larger evergreens in having scented foliage, unless you can count the bitter-almond pungency of the crushed leaves of the common laurel, *Prunus laurocerasus*. The fragrance of the bay leaf is both delicate and elusive and this has proved invaluable where its culinary use is concerned.

The unusual leaf fragrance of box (*Buxus sempervirens*) apparent only when hot sunshine distils the essential oils from its foliage, seems to typify the very essence of a fine summer's day. Not everyone, however, is an admirer of this pungent odour. Queen Anne, for one, is said to have disliked it so intensely that she ordered all the box-edged parterres and knot gardens to be removed from Hampton Court and Kensington Palace.

All the herbs, of course, including thyme, mint, lavender, rosemary, marjoram and, in fact, the whole culinary *bouquet garni* are pleasantly fragrant and most are useful when dried and used as ingredients of potpourri.

The Carolina allspice. Not many plants can claim the triple distinction of scented flowers, leaves and branches, but in the Carolina allspice, *Calycanthus floridus*, the spicy aroma, reminiscent of sandalwood, is present in all three.

My own plant comes from a cutting taken in a derelict Surrey garden. We did not know what it was at the time, but were attracted by the elegant high-gloss foliage. It was five years before it first produced a crop of its curious flowers that look as if they have been cut out of a sheet of slightly tarnished copper. It has travelled with us from one garden to another and is now one of the most treasured occupants of the shrub border. It flowers in June and July.

Chapter Eleven

Town Gardens

A town garden can be anything from a small paved service area, a few yards square, at the rear of the house, to the large plot, surrounded by high brick walls, that is a fast-vanishing feature of our major country towns. Most people who live in towns, however, will have something in between these two extremes to contend with – a smallish garden, enclosed and often surrounded by tall buildings that restrict light and air, and at the same time make it more difficult to obtain the privacy that is one of the *raisons d'être* of any garden, large or small, in town or in country.

The average town garden, then, is likely to be a problem garden. But for those prepared to tackle the problem in a workmanlike manner, the solution can be extremely rewarding. Only a few days before writing this, I had occasion to visit a small Georgian house within the proverbial stone's throw of Chichester cathedral. The pocket garden, little more than a small back yard, could scarcely have measured more than 12 feet in either direction and yet, in that tiny enclosed space, the owners had managed to create an oasis of singular peace and beauty.

The walls had been distempered white to trap and intensify all the light available. In the angle of two of the walls a wrought-iron hay manger served as a container for bright Gustav Emich pelargoniums, their vivid scarlet set off and softened by the silvery leaves of *Senecio cineraria* (*Cineraria maritima*). One wall was covered by a silver-variegated ivy, while in a raised bed, under the watchful eye of a stone cat, blue hydrangeas were massed, with an edging of dwarf ivies and a ground cover of periwinkle. The rest of the area was paved with mellow York stone and that was all. Simple, but very, very effective, and as private and attractive a sitting-out area as anyone could wish for.

Design. Simplicity of design, in fact, should always be the keynote of the small town garden. Within such a restricted area, there is no place for frills and fussing. An appropriate design can make a small garden appear a good deal larger than it really is, and I would advise the owners of such gardens, who are proposing to start from scratch or are contemplating re-planning an existing garden, to avail themselves of the services of a specialist nurseryman or garden designer.

The cost of his services need not be heavy; in fact, the preparation of a planting plan from a description and information supplied by the owner need cost only a guinea or two. To have an expert visit the site to prepare construction and planting plans will obviously be more expensive, but it is a worthwhile outlay which can save a good deal of disappointment and frustration at a later date.

Air pollution. Two major problems are liable to confront the owner of a town garden, particularly if it is in an industrial area. These are atmospheric pollution from smoke and chemical fumes and sour, worn-out soil, whose impoverished condition is aggravated by the two factors just referred to. Fortunately with the increase in legislation relating to smoke abatement and the creation of more and more smokeless zones, the first of these problems is rapidly becoming less acute. Proof of this can be seen in the centres of our largest industrial towns and cities where plants that would not have stood a chance of survival twenty or thirty years ago can be found growing quite happily in centrally situated open spaces and office window-boxes.

In many town districts, however, it is still impossible to grow more than a few types of evergreen or to cultivate successfully the majority of grey and silver-leaved shrubs. Unlike the deciduous shrubs which renew their foliage each spring and shed it during winter, that of the former plants is retained through smog, smoke, snow, hail and sleet when atmospheric pollution and chemical fall-out are at their highest levels.

Soil. The only really effective solution to the problem of sick, worn-out soil is to remove it to a depth of about two spits and replace it completely with good loam or other fertile soil. This, however, is a counsel of perfection, since, all other considerations apart, the majority of town houses are terraced so that an operation of this kind would involve the transportation of large amounts of soil by the only route available, to and fro through the house itself.

Apart from the impracticability of such a proceeding, there is the question of cost, so that it will generally be necessary to settle on a less drastic *modus operandi*. Dressings of lime may do something to counteract soil sickness, but will do little to restore soil fertility. It may be possible, however, to remove just the top 6 inches of soil from the beds and dispose of it elsewhere in the garden, for example, as a foundation for a small raised garden, and bring in fresh soil to replace it. If the soil disposal problem is insoluble, a similar improvement could be effected by surrounding the existing beds with 6-inch brick or stone walls and topping them up with good soil to the new levels. We did this with great success in our London garden, building the beds up with walling stone and importing several loads of Cranleigh loam for the topping-up operation.

Neither of these methods should present a great deal of difficulty in the really small town garden, since the amount of imported soil will not be very large and can be brought through the house in multi-walled paper sacks. Larger town gardens will normally have alternative entrances at the side or rear of the house.

Compost. If none of these cures is feasible, however, regular and generous mulching with peat will generally make a noticeable improvement in the condition and texture of the soil, while fertility can be restored gradually by the use of organic fertilizers such as bonemeal, hoof and horn, shoddy or fish manure, with supplementary dressings of well-rotted garden compost, where the garden is large enough to warrant the inclusion of the invaluable compost bin. I say 'bin' advisedly, since an open heap in a town garden can be a nuisance. Carefully controlled in a properly constructed wooden-slatted bin, garden and household wastes will quickly rot down to a sweet-smelling dark brown crumbly material that is first-rate for rejuvenating tired, worn-out soil.

If there are trees in the garden or its immediate vicinity, the fallen leaves should not be treated as a nuisance, to be raked up and burnt at the first opportunity. They should be jealously hoarded, either for rotting down into leafmould or to use as a valuable surface mulch round choice trees and shrubs.

I know of at least one town gardener who has such a high opinion of the value of these kinds of mulch that he never fails to carry several sacks in the boot of his car on weekend drives to the country and sea. He fills them with dead leaves, leafmould or cut bracken, any of which materials make an excellent summer mulch or, as an addition to the compost heap, greatly improve the texture and fertility of the soil.

Grass. Unless the garden is fairly large, paving is usually to be preferred to grass, particularly if there are children or dogs in the family. This does not mean that the task of making a good turf in a town garden is an impossible one. It will merely involve obtaining seed mixtures suitable for urban conditions, careful attention to preparation of the site and sowing the seed and almost permanent 'Keep off the Grass' notices thereafter if the sward is to be properly maintained.

Paving. Natural stone is the most attractive paving material, and rectangular York slabs look particularly fitted to urban surroundings. They are more expensive than synthetic paving slabs, although the smaller the area to be covered, the less important will be the difference in cost. For the do-it-yourself gardener, however, it will be advisable to remember that the task of laying the natural stone is far more difficult. Slabs of artificial stone are of uniform thickness, while York and other natural paving stones can vary in thickness from $1\frac{1}{2}$ to 3 inches; there is sometimes a difference of an inch in different parts of the same slab, which makes level bedding down a tricky operation.

Brick paving can look very attractive, particularly in association with older buildings. In frosty weather, however, brick paths and terraces can be extremely treacherous to walk on.

Where synthetic paving slabs are used, I would always prefer to restrict my choice to the neutral grey and sand colours. Reds, greens and browns may sound attractive in the brochures, but they tend to give a small garden the checkerboard look of a seaside promenade unless they are used very sparingly.

As a general rule, I would avoid crazy paving in the town garden. I almost finished that last sentence at the word 'paving', but I realize that it still has its attraction for many people and, provided natural stone is employed, crazy paving has a certain fitness for country gardens. In towns, however, its simple, unsophisticated look can be completely out of character.

In certain settings, for the patio or courtyard type of garden, for example, which is a popular feature of contemporary town houses, stone setts or cobbles can look very effective. Although more difficult to come by than they were a few years ago, it is still possible to obtain them. They are easy to lay, either on a screed of concrete, or, where the soil is relatively light and well-drained, on the earth itself.

Leading garden designers have achieved a similar effect, in recent years, by the use of seashore pebbles set in concrete. Geometrical panels of this kind are useful for relieving the monotony of expanses of concrete or synthetic paving.

Flower beds. Provision of space for planting should be generous. The smaller the garden, in fact, the greater should be the proportion of growing space to the remainder of the area. The first impulse will generally be to plant up all the boundaries, but often an effect of greater spaciousness is obtained by having a wide bed on only one of the longer boundaries and by taking the grass or paving practically to the base of the dividing wall or fence at the opposite side, leaving only a narrow strip of border suitable for growing climbers, wall shrubs or hedging.

As much use as possible should be made of the walls of the house itself, and wide beds should be provided at their base to accommodate a variety of climbers and wall shrubs.

Plants for Towns

When we actually come to consider the plants that can be successfully grown in a town garden, we shall discover that the list is surprisingly large. Those with which the greatest difficulty will be experienced will be the grey- and silver-leaved shrubs and perennials, and various evergreens.

But, although the sulphur-laden atmosphere of industrial areas spells death to many of these it can be a positive asset where many of the commoner fungus diseases are concerned. The rose's damask cheek may be sullied by smuts, but her foliage will be free from black spot. Rust diseases of perennials such as hollyhocks and antirrhinums, too, will tend to be far less prevalent.

Bulbs. Bulbs and bedding plants, of course, make first-rate material for the town garden, although some of the bulbs that flourish and increase in the country do little more than hold their own in town. Snowdrops, winter aconites, chionodoxas and scillas, those enthusiastic colonizers of country gardens, will generally be good for only a season or two. Daffodils and narcissus are happy planted in beds, but frequently refuse to naturalize themselves in grass. Crocuses, however, seem to increase just as rapidly in town as elsewhere, although it will frequently be necessary to cotton the flowers as a protection against the depredations of the cockney sparrows.

Bedding plants. Practically all our favourite bedding plants will make a good showing. Zonal pelargoniums (geraniums), fuchsias, begonias, scarlet salvias, china asters, French and African marigolds, ageratum, alyssum, lobelia and heliotrope all do surprisingly well in urban surroundings. Their growth, however, may not be quite so vigorous or their flowers so large.

Wallflowers can be rather dodgy, as they have to stand the winter, but I have found that, where good bushy transplanted stocks are used and put into their flowering positions early – the first half of October is scarcely too soon – the plants will come through to give a worthwhile spring bedding display.

Herbaceous borders. Herbaceous borders are not really suited to the town garden. There are, of course, outstanding examples in urban parks and public gardens, but their success is largely due to there being sufficient space available to site them in sunny open positions. The high walls or fences that shade the majority of long and narrow town plots make it difficult to find a position where the perennial plants can obtain the sunshine and free circulation of air they need if they are not to grow lank and straggly and difficult to support.

One solution of the problem, if space permits, is to use them in an island border towards the centre of the plot and as far away as possible from boundary walls or fences. On the whole, however, it will generally be preferable to use them in groups in association with shrubs in mixed plantings. Grown in this manner, most of the popular perennials will make a satisfactory showing, although we must not expect the plants to have the same size and vigour that they attain in the purer, more open air of the country and outer suburbs.

Best town plants. If I were asked to choose three outstanding plants for the town border, they would be as follows: the bearded or flag iris in all their lovely array of colours, dahlias and fuchsias.

Irises. The iris is a proper townee and will unfurl its elegant flags to perfection in the very heart of industrial towns or other similar urban areas. In such conditions, too, it will usually be found to be free from the unsightly leaf spot which in many gardens makes the green swords look so unsightly after the plants have finished flowering.

Dahlias. Dahlias of all types are seen to perfection in the town garden. Their somewhat garish colours and air of sophistication seems to suit these surroundings. Grown in association with shrubs, they will brighten the garden with their cheerful display, a display that lasts from early July until mid-November, thanks to the later incidence of frost in town gardens.

Fuchsias. Fuchsias, too, have that air of sophistication that seems to fit them for duty in town. Some, such as *F. magellanica* 'Riccartonii', are almost completely hardy; others like the crimson and coral-red *F. parviflora*, the trailing New Zealand species *F. procumbens* and named hybrids such as Brilliant (rosy-scarlet and purple), Display (carmine and rose-pink) and Elsa (violet-rose and pink) may be cut to ground level in severe winters. The pink and white Mrs W. P. Wood and the dwarf cerise and mauve Tom Thumb are two of the numerous fully hardy varieties.

Buddleia. Most hardy deciduous shrubs will prove satisfactory, including deciduous species of barberry, cotoneaster and viburnum. *Buddleia davidii*, as might be expected, is very much at home in the town garden. It was this, together with the rose bay willow herb, that colonized city bomb sites during the Second World War.

Aucuba. Some evergreens seem to be able to put up with the smoke and chemical-laden atmosphere of industrial areas. Spotted laurel, *Aucuba japonica* 'Maculata', a fugitive from the Victorian shrubbery, has staged an urban comeback, thanks to its powers of resistance to smog. It also makes a good town hedging plant. Others that seem equally happy in 'the smoke' are box, ivies, hollies, pyracantha and, of course, privet, the golden forms of which, grown individually, make quite handsome specimen shrubs.

In winter, the leaves of evergreens tend to become grimy and soot-encrusted. It is worth while giving them an occasional vigorous syringing with clean water. This not only does wonders for their appearance but also allows them to breathe more freely the precious carbon dioxide so vital to the metabolism of all green plants.

Roses. Roses of all kinds, generally speaking, do well in towns and look particularly effective when grown in beds set in areas of paving. On trellises and pergolas they are useful for screening purposes, and serve a useful decorative function on the walls of the house itself. Mermaid and New Dawn, which I described in Chapter Nine (p 113), are two among many that can be strongly recommended for this last purpose.

For bedding, it will be better to avoid the more vigorous, tall-growing hybrid teas and floribundas such as Peace and Queen Elizabeth and many of their numerous offspring and descendants. There is just no room in the average town garden to accommodate these lanky six-footers, particularly in bedding arrangements.

Six feet, in fact is a conservative estimate for many of these new giants. A rose-growing friend who exhibits at all the important shows, told me only the other day that he has to look out of his bedroom windows to see whether there are any

Queen Elizabeths suitable for showing!

Shelter. The provision of shelter, privacy and a pleasant sitting-out area will form the major priorities in any plan for a town garden. Even more than in rural districts, where peace abounds in the neighbouring countryside, is it essential to have such a haven of refuge from the noise and turmoil of the streets outside.

The fortunate owner of a walled garden is already halfway towards the achievement of this aim. He will only have to select a corner where two walls meet, sheltered from the north and east, in which to provide a paved area for garden chairs and a table. It is an easy matter to decorate the walls with climbers and brighten up the terrace a little with plants in urns or tubs, with perhaps a stone or lead figure or a mini-pool with fountain thrown in for good measure.

Hedges. But where wooden fences or interlap screens are used to divide the garden from its neighbours, and this is the usual pattern of modern urban house design, it will be better to supplement them with a living screen that will act also as a shelter and windbreak. It is difficult to find suitable hedging plants to provide complete privacy, but the much-maligned privet will do the job as well as any other.

Privet. The oval-leaved privet, *Ligustrum ovalifolium*, is the species most commonly grown. Both the type and the golden-leaved variety, 'Aureum', can make an attractive and close-knit hedge provided they are kept neatly trimmed. Town-dwellers should forget any prejudices they may have against this useful shrub, as far as their hedging requirements are concerned.

One of the worst criticisms to be levelled against privet hedges is that they need clipping every other week or so during their growing season. This need no longer be a cause for complaint as there is now a spray available which inhibits summer growth and reduces clipping to a minimum.

In addition to the oval-leaved species there is one that is less common, *L. lucidum*, which is equally happy in soot-laden atmospheres. With its larger, lustrous green leaves it makes a much more handsome hedging plant than the former.

The white, lilac-type flowers, 8 inches in length, are quite striking and are followed by blue-black berries. There are two interesting varieties, 'Aureum Variegatum', with opaque yellow foliage and 'Excelsum Superbum', whose large green leaves are beautifully marbled with white, yellow and silver.

Ligustrum lucidum needs less severe treatment than the oval-leaved form where clipping is concerned. It responds most satisfactorily to an annual light going over in spring.

Firethorns. *Pyracantha atalantioides* makes an attractive evergreen hedge, with its long glossy oval leaves and abundance of foamy white flower clusters in June. One of its main attractions is its berries, which are deep red and borne in large clusters. Those of this particular species are not very attractive to birds and will remain on the plants until the New Year. Light pruning, cutting back the fruiting sprays in late winter or early spring will ensure a lavish display.

Pyracantha watereri is another excellent hedging kind with an even denser habit of growth. It is covered, at the appropriate seasons, with masses of white blossom and a blaze of scarlet berries.

Cotoneasters. Our very first garden, back in the Thirties, was a town garden and we considered ourselves very advanced in planting a hedge of the scarlet-berried *Cotoneaster simonsii*. Although only a semi-evergreen, it compensates for this by the brilliance of its autumn foliage and it was a welcome change from the ubiquitous privet with which we were surrounded. I can vouch for its success as a town hedging plant. It grew so thickly that within a year or so we had to remove alternate plants and it never failed to yield a bumper crop of scarlet boot-button berries.

Since then, I have grown many other cotoneasters that are more showy and less common, but I shall always have a soft spot for *C. simonsii*; when seedlings appear in the cottage garden as they do, from time to time, from plants that have naturalized themselves in the surrounding woodland, I have not the heart to throw them away, and those that I cannot dispose of to gardening friends are carefully planted in a corner of the shrub borders, or in one of the wilder parts of the garden.

Climbers. Privacy can be increased by topping-up walls or fences with trellis and covering it with climbers like wisteria, clematis and honeysuckle, the foliage of which will provide screening when it is most needed.

It is obvious, therefore, that, provided we are willing to accept its limitations and strive as far as possible to overcome them, there is no reason why even the most dedicated gardener should not be able to obtain a full measure of enjoyment from a garden in town.

Chapter Twelve

Garden Gallimaufry

Nobody would deny that it is the living material – the shrubs, trees, plants and bulbs – that are primarily responsible for the appeal of a garden. But 'accessories', a word more commonly associated with the fashion magazines than with horticultural journals, can still play an important part towards the success of any garden. They are, in effect, the icing on the cake, the olive in the martini.

When gardeners talk of accessories, they are generally thinking in terms of tubs, urns, vases, sundials, statues and birdbaths, all of which are useful in providing additional garden interest, particularly during those few barren winter months when there is little else to attract.

Tubs. Pots and tubs, planted with flowers, shrubs or even small trees, enhance the interest of terraces and paved areas. Today, there is ample choice of materials and design. Tubs are perhaps the most widely used type of container and take the form of barrels cut in half or specially made wooden containers, circular or rectangular in shape, constructed usually of oak staves banded with iron.

Such tubs as these are ideal for shrubs, while the largest sizes will accommodate – for a number of years at least – slow-growing trees and conifers. Before they are planted up, precautions against rot and decay ought to be taken. There are two ways of preventing deterioration; by painting the inside with a non-toxic paint or a non-toxic wood preservative that will not harm the plants.

Drainage holes must be provided in the bottom, about 6 inches apart and not less than $\frac{1}{2}$ inch in diameter. A bit, sufficiently large to make holes of this size, is not likely to form part of many home carpenters' equipment. Failing this, however, the holes can be made with a red hot poker.

When the tubs are in use, the bases should stand clear of the ground. Bricks or blocks of wood can be used for this purpose. The tubs should be painted a colour that does not clash either with their living contents or with their architectural surroundings. The paint colour known as 'Wimbledon' green is generally considered suitable for garden use, although I would not agree (see p 49). For most gardens, and certainly for terraces, I would prefer to use white or off-white, with the bands picked out in black.

Composts. It is important to use suitable composts for filling the containers, particularly where permanent or semi-permanent subjects are being grown. John Innes No 2 suits most flowers and geraniums, petunias, begonias, fuchsias, lilies and other similar tub and pot plants will thrive in it, but for shrubs and small trees I find a mixture of 2 parts loam to 1 part peat and 1 part bonfire ash, generously laced with bonemeal, much more satisfactory.

I grow hydrangeas, clipped box and sweet bay in this manner and every two or three years the top half of the soil is carefully removed and replaced with fresh mixture.

Ample provision for drainage must be made, whether the containers are of wood or other material, such as stone, concrete or clay. A 2-inch layer of broken crocks should cover the bottom, with a further 2 or 3 inches of coarse material, such as chopped turf or the coarse siftings of the compost heap on top of this. This is topped up with the mixture described above. In many instances, it may be better to rest the tree or shrub on the layer of coarse material and work compost gently round its roots – or round the root-ball in the case of evergreens and conifers – firming it with a dibber. Do not forget to leave a clear inch at the top to simplify watering operations. Remember, too, to fill the tub in the position in which it is going to stand. Large containers filled with earth are ton weights and need rollers to move them.

Other containers. In addition to wooden containers there are various other types, some of natural or synthetic stone, often elegantly carved with swags and festoons of leaves and flowers, or embossed with classical or Tudor designs. Lead tanks, cisterns and urns are delightful to look at, but cripplingly expensive to buy; reproductions in fibreglass, authentic down to the attractive patina acquired by lead after years of weathering, are now obtainable at prices within the reach of everyone. Glazed Italian terracotta pots, looking rather like grandmother's breadbin in green, blue, and cream glazes are cheap and extremely effective for small shrubs such as camellias and hydrangeas. Concrete containers, like very deep saucers, which made their first appearance at the Festival of Britain, are becoming increasingly popular and suit to perfection the austere style of contemporary architecture. They will take anything from scarlet salvias to silver birch.

Urns look best at or above eye level, on walls or specially built plinths or pillars flanking flights of steps. They make the perfect receptacle for ivy-leaved geraniums or other trailing plants. Petunias, too, can look extremely attractive in them, while in spring, they are useful for hyacinths.

Italian wine jars in terracotta are attractive architecturally but of little use for planting on account of their narrow necks. Strawberry barrels enjoyed a tremendous popularity for several years; plants are put in the top and also in holes drilled round the circumference. Bumper crops of fruit were promised, but everyone I know who tried them was disappointed. Apparently watering was a problem and crops did not come up to expectations. Perhaps that is why we hear much less about them nowadays.

Ornaments. When anyone attempts to discuss garden ornaments and statues, he is treading on dangerous ground. Britain is still a democracy and everyone is entitled to indulge his own fancies even to the extent of cramming his garden full of nauseating gnomes, deadly dwarfs and outsize spotted toadstools. May I, however, make a plea for a little self-discipline where these are concerned. Even costly statues of impeccable taste can look completely out of place in unsuitable surroundings. We must be doubly careful, therefore, that our more humble garden ornaments are in keeping with the design and layout of our gardens, and gnomes and coy animals seldom are.

Stone figures, sundials and birdbaths need be neither grotesquely Disneyish or madly expensive. A few weeks ago, we picked up a delightful seventeenth-century stone cherub – who has, incidentally, been christened Fred – for almost the proverbial song. He was standing forlornly outside an antique shop in Billingshurst, having just been evicted from a stately home in the neighbourhood.

Anyone who keeps his eyes open on his weekend travels and at auction sales should be able to pick up similar pieces at reasonable prices. Remember, however, that a little of this sort of thing goes a very long way in the small garden.

Garden centres. This book, I feel, would scarcely be complete without at least a passing mention of the garden centres that are springing up all over the countryside like mushrooms. These are the horticultural equivalent of the self-service store, where plants of every kind are spread out temptingly for the customers to take away with them. Garden centres can be a boon to the novice and the less knowledgeable gardener. They can see just what they are getting and meet in the flesh (not quite the correct expression!) plants that previously they have encountered only between the pages of garden books and periodicals.

Attached to reliable nurseries, garden centres are an unmixed blessing. But about some of the others, I would not be quite so enthusiastic. They are run, in some instances, by people with little or no horticultural experience and no real love for plants, whose only idea is to jump on the band wagon and cash in on the current gardening boom. Stocks are bought-in from outside and plants in containers for taking away are not always well looked after, particularly during the summer months. Buying from them becomes a hit-or-miss sort of business, with the possibility of a high percentage of failures, to say nothing of the introduction of inferior and commonplace types of plant to our gardens. Although the garden centre reflects the spirit of the times, it is a trend that an old garden diehard like me would not care to see developing much further. Many of the leading nurserymen to whom I have spoken are of a similar opinion.

Nurserymen. Talking of nurserymen reminds me that it is time that someone said a few words in defence of that much-criticized body of men. I doubt whether there is a finer group of businessmen – and they *are* businessmen and not philanthropists, as many of their customers appear to think – operating throughout the length and breadth of Britain.

Believe me, I have no personal axe to grind in this connexion except that some of my best friends are nurserymen.

Ordering plants. There are six golden rules that the prospective customer might like to bear in mind when sending in his order.

1. Send it in good time – in early summer if possible. The earlier you send it the more prompt will be the delivery with a much greater chance of getting everything you order. Plants are not like most other commodities – suppliers cannot suddenly produce more to order.

2. Whenever possible, deal from a reliable local nursery and try to collect your order. This will not only ensure that you get plants that suit your local conditions, it will also save the nurseryman a great deal of trouble and you will save the cost of packing and delivery – a not inconsiderable item nowadays.

3. If you are not sure whether the plants you are ordering are

> (*a*) hardy
> (*b*) suitable for your particular soil and situation

write and inquire before ordering. Reputable nurseries will be only too happy to advise you.

4. *Do* make proper preparations for the new arrivals. Where trees and shrubs form part of the order, have planting holes ready. Do not try to plant when the soil is frozen concrete-hard or when it is waterlogged after heavy rainfall. Heel the plants in until weather and soil conditions improve. They will come to no harm in a trench provided the roots are completely covered with earth.

5. Do not panic if your order does not arrive with the first autumn frosts. Nurseries lift from the end of October until the end of March and the planting of most trees, shrubs and

herbaceous plants can be safely carried out at any time during that period, given suitable weather conditions. Some plants, such as evergreens and conifers, however, are best left until April, if they cannot be got in by mid-November.

6. Write and tell your nurseryman about any complete failures. Let him know just what happened to them and what treatment you gave them, etc. Many nurseries, provided you can satisfy them that failure was not due to your own carelessness in planting and cultivation, should replace such plants, if not free, at least at a reduced charge. They want you to be satisfied, it is the customers' goodwill that makes their businesses prosper.

Index

PAN SELECTION OF GARDENING

THE SMALL GREENHOUSE	H. Witham Fogg	40p
THE KITCHEN GARDEN (illus)	Brian Furner	30p
ROSES AND THEIR CULTIVATION	Edited by P. Hunt	50p
GARDEN SHRUBS AND TREES	,, ,,	50p
GREENHOUSE AND INDOOR PLANTS	,, ,,	50p
FRUIT AND VEGETABLES	,, ,,	50p
SHRUBS AND TREES FOR SMALL GARDENS	Christopher Lloyd	40p
ROSES FOR SMALL GARDENS (illus)	C.E. Lucas Phillips	40p
THE SMALL GARDEN (illus)	,, ,,	40p

These and other PAN Books are obtainable from all book-sellers and newsagents. If you have any difficulty please send purchase price plus 5p postage to P.O. Box 11, Falmouth, Cornwall.

While every effort is made to keep prices low, it is sometimes neccessary to increase prices at short notice. PAN Books reserve the right to show new retail prices on covers which may differ from those advertised in the text or elsewhere.